A Study of General Epistles

VOLUME 1
James • First Peter • Second Peter

by Billy W. Moore

More than a workbook - a Bible study book!
A paragraph by paragraph, verse by verse study!

ONE STONE
BIBLICAL RESOURCES

Published by:
One Stone Press
979 Lovers Lane
Bowling Green, KY 42103

Printed in the United States of America

ISBN 10: 1-941422-26-8
ISBN 13: 978-1-941422-26-7

ONE STONE
BIBLICAL RESOURCES

www.onestone.com

To our granddaughter Rachel Elyse Moore:

May she grow up to be one of the "Holy Women"

as Sarah, the grandmother-in-law of Rachel, her namesake.

How to Use This Book

This book is designed to help the Bible student come to a better understanding of the Scriptures by directing the student to the word of God for answers and by giving pertinent comments by others who have put many years into studying the word. All comments, my own and others, are offered as a help and are not to be taken as the scriptures.

The lessons cannot be studied without reading the scripture. This is not a substitute for The Word, but an assist to those who desire to study the Word, and we trust that it shall be helpful to those who spend the hours that will be required to complete the lessons in this series.

In teaching these lessons I encourage each student to prepare the lesson before coming to class; I encourage teachers at the beginning of each class period to have a reading of the text to be studied in that period; and to call upon members of the class to read a question, supply the answer, and follow with discussion.

This series of lessons is not prepared for a definite period of time. It was not arranged for one lesson each class period, but it is designed for a "verse by verse," "paragraph by paragraph" study of the word of God. We have placed "headings," or "paragraph content" at the beginning of each paragraph. These constitute a sort of "index" for the book being studied. We encourage the student to make an index for each book, for this will help one to keep in mind the specific subject matter of each book. Then when you call a book to mind, you will also know why that epistle was written, with what it deals, etc. This is a great help in the overall study of the Scripture.

— *Author*

Introduction

It should be the desire of every child of God to "grow in grace and knowledge of our Lord and Savior Jesus Christ" (2 Peter 3: 18). Those who have endeavored to grow can look back over their years and recall their increase in knowledge of the Word. Yet, as we read and study, we realize how much more there is to learn of our Lord; as we listen to others who have applied themselves to study and learning of Jesus, we are made to realize our own need to increase our knowledge, and when we learn from others, there is the desire to share.

In teaching Bible classes in Butler, Missouri, we have made outlines and questions of the books of the New Testament and provided them for the classes. It was decided to provide a more thorough study of The Epistle of James, then 1 Peter and 2 Peter. In preparing these lessons several different commentaries were used, with pertinent quotations given in the printed material, so the student would have these comments (all students do not have access to the various commentaries on each book of the Bible). These lessons were then used by my brother, Don Moore, who was preaching for the Affton, Missouri church. He and the classes there enjoyed and appreciated the material, which provoked a similar effort with the Epistles of John and Jude.

This is not just a workbook. It is a study of the text itself. But even more, it contains many quotations from W. E. Vine, Joseph Henry Thayer, Adam Clarke, Roy E. Cogdill, R. C. H. Llenski, James McKnight, Guy N. Woods, E. M. Zerr, and many others. It is designed to help the student better understand some rather difficult passages by giving opinions of several others on these texts. It can also provide help for the teacher, who often desires to have access to a greater source of material when he prepares to teach a class in a "verse by verse" study, and that is just what this study is: a verse by verse, subject by subject, paragraph by paragraph study of these General Epistles; although some may classify II John and III John as being written to specific persons rather than General Epistles, they are included in these studies.

Our lives have been blessed and enriched with six grandchildren and we hope they shall always desire to walk with the Lord. If our studies and writings can help them and other Christians to "walk in the light, as he is in the light," to be more aware of "the doctrine of Christ," to "add to their faith, virtue, knowledge, temperance, patience, godliness, brotherly kindness and love," so they can have eternal life with our Lord and Savior, all the efforts shall be worthwhile. To this end these lessons have been prepared.

— *Author*

Bibliography

Vine, W. E., *Expository Dictionary of New Testament Words*, Fleming H. Revell Company, Westwood, N.J., Thirteenth impression 1964.

Thayer, Joseph Henry, *Greek-English Lexicon of the New Testament*, Zondervan Publishing House, Grand Rapids, Michigan, 1963 printing.

Clarke, Adam, *Clark's Commentary, Volume VI, The New Testament of our Lord and Savior Jesus Christ, Volume II. Romans to the Revelations.* Abingdon-Cokesbury Press, New York – Nashville.

Cogdill, Roy E., *The New Testament: Book By Book*, Cogdill Foundation Publications, Marion, Indiana.

Lenski, R. C. H., *The Interpretation of Epistles of I and II Peter, the Three Epistles of John, And the Epistle of Jude*, Augsburg Publishing House, Minneapolis, Minnesota, 1961.

MacKnight on the Epistles, Baker Book House, Grand Rapids, Michigan, Reprinted 1984, One-Volume Edition.

Woods, Guy N., *A Commentary on the Epistle of James*, Gospel Advocate Company, Nashville, Tennessee, 1964 edition.

---, *A Commentary on the New Testament Epistles of Peter, John, and Jude*, Gospel Advocate Company, Nashville, Tennessee, 1954.

Zerr, E. M., *Zerr Bible Commentary, Volume Six*, Cogdill Foundation, Marion, Indiana.

Reference Symbols

C—Cogdill

L—Lenski

M—MacKnight

W—Woods

Z—Zerr

V—Vine

T—Thayer

NASB—New American Standard Bible

NKJV—New King James Version

Table of Contents

THE SECOND EPISTLE OF PETER

The Epistle of James: Chapter 1

ABOUT THE EPISTLE OF JAMES

Unlike the letters written by Paul, which were directed either to individual Christians or congregations of Christians in some particular locality, the Epistle of James is one of the general epistles of the New Testament, addressed to no particular individual and to no particular congregation, but to the church which had been dispersed. In the epistle the address James uses to designate those to whom he is writing is "the twelve tribes which are scattered abroad, " or "which are of the Dispersion, greeting" (1:1).

The epistle of James is of an intensely practical nature and is primarily concerned with the ethics of Christian living and service. With the writer of this epistle religion was not a matter of theory and speculation, as was true of many of the false religions in New Testament days, but it was a matter of revealed truth which was intended to be the guide for the life of the individual. The book emphasizes truth as it is meant to be expressed in Christian living and in the performance of Christian duty. Some have called it "the gospel of common sense" (C—140).

THE AUTHOR

At the beginning of the letter the writer identifies himself as "James, a servant of God and of the Lord Jesus Christ" (1:1). This does not, however, identify the author in a very definite way. In the New Testament there are at least four men by the name of James:

1. The brother of John and son of Zebedee was called James (Matt. 10:2). He was killed by Herod Agrippa I early in the history of the church (Acts 12:1-2).

2. Another of the disciples of Jesus bore the name of James (Matt. 10:3), and he is further identified as the son of Alphaeus.

3. There was then a James, who was the brother of Judas, another one of Jesus' disciples (Luke 6:16). This Judas is distinguished from Judas Iscariot who betrayed the Lord (Luke 6:16).

4. There was James who was the brother of Jesus, being one of the four brothers of the Lord (Matt. 13:55).

It is not likely that the Epistle of James was written by James, the son of Zebedee and the brother of John, for the reason that this James met an early death, earlier perhaps than the writing of the letter. Neither is it likely that James, the Son of Alphaeus, could have written the Epistle, or did write it, because we know very little about him and he is rather obscure in the New Testament history except for his identification as one of the Apostles. The probability is, and it is commonly accepted, that James, the brother of our Lord, is the author of the Epistle of James.

Josephus tells us that James was stoned by the order of Anannias, the high priest, but Eusebius said that he was thrust down from the pinnacle of the Temple and then beaten to death with a club. These are traditions concerning the end of his life as a servant of the Lord, and we do not know whether or not they are true.

The New Testament: Book by Book, pages 140-141. Cogdill Foundation Publication. Note: I commend this book, *A 26 Lesson Outline Series Covering the Entire New Testament*. It contains valuable information regarding each of the 26 books.

THE EPISTLE OF JAMES

Introduction: The writer was probably James, the brother of the Lord (Matt. 13:55) who continued with the disciples after the resurrection and ascension of Christ (Acts 1:14). (See comments by Cogdill above.)

Before attempting to work this lesson, read the book of James. It will be even better if you will read it a second time and try to determine the purpose of writing the letter. Remember, we are studying a letter written more than 1,900 years ago, to people who had different customs than ours, who spoke a different language than ours. The letter was written in a language they understood. We must have a translation of the letter into the English. The more we learn of the times in which they lived, the better we may be able to understand the letter that was written to them.

THE WRITER AND THOSE TO WHOM HE WROTE (VS. 1-2)

1.   How does the writer identify himself? _____

      a. Are all Christians servants of the Lord? _____

2.   To whom was the letter written? _____

Note: The children of Israel, the twelve tribes of Israel, also called the Jews, were God's chosen people from the days of Israel unto the establishing of the church. Sometimes the word Jew or Israel is used in a figurative sense, denoting the people of God, not the fleshly descendants of Israel. Here are some examples:

    a. Who is a Jew, according to Romans 2:28-29? _____

    b. How did Paul refer to God's people in Galatians 6:16? _____

    c. Can you now see how "the twelve tribes" refers to the chosen people of God? _____

    d. Where were those people? _____

         What caused them to be "scattered abroad" (See Acts 8:1)? _____

         _____

         How did James refer to them? _____

LET'S TALK ABOUT TEMPTATION (VS. 2-16)

1.   Define temptation. _____

     _____

2.   When did James tell brethren to "count it all joy"? _____

     _____

3.   What is accomplished by the trying of your faith (3)? _____

     _____

4.   Read Hebrews 10:36 and tell what we all need. _____

     _____

5.   What did James say we should "ask of God" (5)? _____

     _____

     Why do we need wisdom in time of temptation? _____

     _____

6.   How should we ask of God (6)? _____

     What does "nothing wavering" mean? (See NASB on this verse.) _____

     _____

7.   What kind of man can receive nothing of the Lord (7)? _____

     _____

8. What lesson is taught by the reference to the grass and the flower of the grass (9-11)? _____

9. What blessing will be given to those who endure temptation (12)?

   _____

10. Can God be tempted with evil (13)? _____
    Does He tempt us with evil? _____

11. How is a man tempted (14-15)? _____

    _____

12. Read Matthew 4:1-11, which tells of the temptation of Jesus.

    a. What did Jesus call to mind each time He was tempted? _____

    b. Can we overcome temptation by following the example of Christ? Examples (supply the scriptures that would help us overcome):

       (1) When tempted to lie _____

       (2) When tempted to steal _____

       (3) When tempted to drink strong drink _____

       (4) When tempted to commit adultery _____

    c. Can we overcome temptation as Jesus did if we do not know what is written? _____
       Do you see why it is important to read the scripture? _____
       What can you do to help others learn the word of God? _____

       _____

       How can parents or grandparents help children learn the word?

       _____

       What does the local church do to help us learn the word? _____

       _____

BLESSINGS FROM GOD (VS. 17-18)

1. Read verse 17 and tell what has come from God. _____

   _____

   a. Do you really believe this? _____

    b.   How did James describe God? _____

_____

2.   James says God "begat" us. What does "begat" mean? _____

    a.   How has God done this? _____

    b.   Why has God done this? _____

    c.   Is this a blessing from God (1 John 3:1)? _____

    d.   How did Paul say he had begotten those at Corinth (1 Cor. 4:15)?

_____

    e.   A birth follows a begetting. Read 1 Peter 1:23 and tell of what
God's people are born. _____
When one hears the gospel of Christ and believes, he is begotten.
When that believer is baptized he is born again, "born of water
and of the Spirit" (John 3:3-5) and is saved (Mark 16:16). Do you
see why one must hear the gospel before he can be saved? _____

    f.   James said, of those First Century Christians, "that we should be
a kind of _____ of his creatures."
What is first-fruits? _____
Can we be "fruits" of his creatures? _____

HEARING AND DOING (VS. 19-25)

1.   How should we be about hearing (19)? _____

2.   In what two things should we be slow? _____

3.   Why should we be slow to wrath (20)? _____

_____

    a.   Does this mean that anger does not help one to do God's will?_____

    b.   Read Ephesians 4:26 and tell what Paul says about being angry.

_____

What are some sins that may be committed because of anger?

_____

4.   What are we told to "lay apart" (21)? _____
     Compare the NASB and NKJV and see what words are used. _____

     _____

5.   What are we to receive (hear) with meekness (21)? _____

     _____

6.   What is the word of God able to do (21)? _____

     _____

     a.   Read Acts 20:32, a part of Paul's farewell address to brethren at
          Miletus. What did he commend unto them? _____
          What did he say the word is able to do?_____
          Can you see why you should get to know the word of God?_____

7.   How do people often deceive themselves (22)? _____

     _____

8.   The man who is a hearer of the word and not a doer is compared to
     what? (23-24) _____

     a.   Is it wrong for one to look at himself in a mirror? _____
          Then what does this mean?_____

          _____

9.   What three things must one do to "be blessed in his deeds" (25)?

     a.   _____

     b.   _____

     c.   _____

     Question: are you doing these three things? _____

PURE RELIGION (VS. 26-27)

1.   James speaks of a man whose religion is vain (26).

     a.   What is religion? _____

     b.   What does "vain" mean?_____
          Then, is it possible that some religions will accomplish nothing in

so far as eternal salvation is concerned? _____

c. What two things are said of this man who seems to be religious?

(1) _____

(2) _____

d. What does it mean to bridle the tongue?_____

_____

e. How does one sometimes deceive himself (22)? _____

_____

Would you conclude that the man who is a hearer, but not a doer of the word, has a vain religion? _____

2. Let's talk about the religion that is pure and undefiled (27).

a. What two things must this include?

(1) _____

(2) _____

Note: James is not saying that these two things are all that is required to practice pure religion. This is a figure of speech where one thing, or, in this instance, two things, are put for the whole. Other things are involved in pure religion: faith in God, repenting, confessing sins, praying, worshipping in spirit and in truth, living soberly, living righteously, living godly, etc. But one's religion cannot be pure in the absence of these two.

b. When does he say they visit the fatherless and the widows?

_____

c. What does it mean to visit them? Does it mean just to go see them? _____

If not, tell what it means. _____

_____

d. Is this an opportunity to do unto others as you would have them do unto you? _____

e. What does it mean to keep "unspotted from the world"?_____

_____

f.   What is there of the world that can "spot" the Christian? (Read 1 John 2:15-17). List the three things:

(1) _____

(2) _____

(3) _____

g.   Read John 15:18-19 and tell the relationship of the disciple of Christ to the world. _____

_____

h.   How can you keep unspotted? _____

_____

3.   Is practicing pure and undefiled religion something each Christian must do?_____

Can the local church do this for you? _____

Some seem to think that if the local church makes contributions to some benevolent organization that engages in the care of children or widows, they would have no obligation. Do you agree? _____

4.   If James 1:27 authorizes church sponsored children's homes or widows' homes, then would Matthew 25:35-36 authorize church sponsored hospitals? _____

Clothing stores? _____ Jails? _____ If not, why not? ___

_____

_____

The Epistle of James: Chapter 2

RESPECTER OF PERSONS—THE RICH AND THE POOR (VS. 1-13)

1. What does respecter of persons mean? _____
    _____

2. Is God a respecter of persons (Acts 10:34-35)? _____

3. What were they not to have or to hold with respect of persons? _____
    _____
    Had some showed respect of persons regarding this? _____

4. Describe the two men used in the illustration of being a respecter of persons. _____
    _____

5. How was respect of persons showed for the man who wore the costly clothing? _____

6. How was the poor man treated? _____

7. Because of the different treatment given to the rich man and the poor man, what conclusion was reached (4)? _____
    _____

8. How do many people still show special treatment for the rich? _____
    _____

9. Discuss the rich and the poor (5-7).

    a. Who has God chosen of this world (5)? _____

    b. In what are they rich? _____
        What does this mean? _____

    c. Of what are they heirs? _____

    d. Can you see that there are "poor – rich" people? _____

    e.   Are there any "rich – poor" people? _____
        How would you describe them? _____

    f.   Could there be some "rich – rich" people? _____
        How would you describe them? _____

    g.   Are there any "poor – poor" people? _____
        Who are they? _____

    h.   From this point of view how do you think God would describe
        you? _____

10.   How did some brethren feel toward the poor (6)? _____
_____
Do some still feel this way? _____

11.   How did rich people treat the people of God (6-7)? _____
_____

    a.   Read Acts 8:1 and 9:1 and tell how the church was treated. _____
        _____
        Were some of the rich doing this? _____

    b.   What had Jesus told his disciples regarding this (Luke 21:12)?
        _____

    c.   Read Acts 4:18-21; 5:17-28. Was that which Jesus forewarned now
        coming to pass? _____

12.   What is "that worthy name" by which disciples of Christ were called
    (Acts 11:26)? _____

    a.   What should be the attitude of one who suffers because he is a
        Christian (1 Peter 4:16)? _____

13.   How does James refer to the law of Christ (8)? _____
    Peter referred to the people of God as a priesthood (1 Peter 2:9).
    What kind of priesthood?_____

14.   What is said of one who will love his neighbor as himself (8)? _____
_____

Would it be just as well not to love your neighbor? _____

15. What two things are said of the one who has respect to persons (9)?

_____

_____

16. What is said of one who keeps the whole law and yet offends in one point? _____

17. How should we speak and do (12)? _____

_____

18. What is the law of liberty (12, Cf. 1:25)? _____

19. The need of mercy:

a. What is mercy? _____

b. Who will have judgment without mercy (13)? _____

c. Do we all sin or offend in some points? _____

d. Do we all need the mercy of God at the judgment? _____

e. Should we show mercy unto others? _____

FAITH AND WORKS (VS. 14-26)

1. What question is raised in verse fourteen? _____

2. Let's talk about faith:

a. What is faith (Heb. 11:1)? _____
    Note: There are two facets of faith, one is conviction and the
    other is confidence.

b. How does faith come (Rom. 10:17)? _____

c. How does faith relate to pleasing God (Heb. 11:6)? _____

_____

d. Read Mark 16:16 and tell what the Lord said of one who does not
    believe. _____

    e. By what are we justified (Rom. 5:1)? _____

    f.   Read Galatians 5:6 and tell the kind of faith that avails. _____

        _____

    g. Paul said, "For by _____ are ye saved through _____ "
        (Eph. 2:8).

    h. Do all of these references warrant the conclusion that we are
        saved "by faith"? _____

    i.   Do any of these scriptures say we are saved by "faith only"?_____

    j.   Can one have conviction that God is, and that Jesus is the Son of
        God and not obey the Lord? Before answering, read John 12:42.

        _____

    k. Is it safe to conclude that there are different kinds or degrees of
        faith?_____

3.   A study of works: There are different kinds of works mentioned in the
    Bible. Some make no distinction between these kinds of works and
    conclude that all works are excluded from salvation by grace. They
    say we are "saved by grace" through faith, "not of works", therefore
    baptism is not necessary to salvation, for it is a work. Read the
    scriptures and see the different kinds of works and learn what kinds
    of works are excluded in "salvation by grace."

    a. Works of the law of Moses (Gal. 2:16). Are we saved by this kind of
        work? _____

    b. Meritorious works (Eph. 2:8-9). Meritorious means "deserving
        reward or praise" (*American Heritage Dictionary*). Are we saved by
        this kind of work?_____

    c.   Works of man's own righteousness (Rom. 10:1-3). Are we saved by
        this kind of work?_____

    d. Works of God (John 6:28; 9:3-4). Are these works excluded from
        our salvation?_____

e. Works of righteousness (Acts 10:34-35). Is this kind of work absolutely essential to man's salvation?_____
    Note: Can you see that there are different kinds of works mentioned in the Bible? If not, then read the preceding scriptures again. If yes, then continue the questions in this lesson.

4. Two questions are asked in verse 14, what are they?

    a. _____
        Does it profit anyone for one to say he has faith but has not works?_____

    b. _____
        Compare the NASB and the NKJV on this verse. "That kind of faith"—faith without works—cannot save. Saving faith includes works of righteousness, or works of obedience to God.

5. In the rest of this chapter there are five illustrations which show that "faith, if it does not have works is dead," it cannot save. What example is used in verses 15-16?_____
    _____

    a. Does it help a brother who is hungry if you say to him, " Brother I am a believer too, I hope things go better for you"? If he is cold, does it help him just to say, "I have faith"? What does it take to help a brother or sister who is hungry?_____
        What about one who is cold and naked?_____

6. What conclusion is drawn after this example (17)?_____
    _____

    a. Can one be saved by a dead faith?_____

    b. What is the opposite of a "dead" faith?_____
        Would this be the same as "faith which worketh by love" (Gal. 5:6)?
        _____

7. What did James ask of the one who says, "You have faith, and I have works" (18)?_____

a.   Is it possible for one to show his faith without any works? _____
Note: James is not saying that one can show his faith without any
works, but just the opposite. He is saying you cannot show your
faith without doing anything. We must be careful that we do not
make a complete separation of "faith" and "works." "Faith" is not
something off over here (on the left) and "works" something over
here (on the right), as if they are completely separated and in
order to be saved we must join the two.

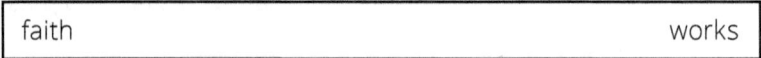

faith	works

No! James is saying, you do not have saving faith in the absence
of works. The following example shows the kind of works to which
he is referring.

b.   How did James say, "I will show you my faith" (18)? _____
_____
James is saying saving faith and works are inseparable. Do you
see that?

8.   The devils are used to illustrate that "faith without works" will not
save. Do the devils believe there is one God? _____
What else do the devils do in addition to believing? _____
What does it mean when he says they tremble? _____
_____

a.   If one believes there is one God but does not work (do) the
commandments of God, is he any better off than the devils?_____
Are the devils going to be saved eternally? _____
Then what of the man who only believes? _____

9.   How did James refer to the man who only believes (20)? _____
(NKJV says "foolish"). What does "vain" mean? _____

a.   What did James say about "faith without works" (20)? _____

b.   Would you want to meet the Lord in judgment with that kind of
faith? _____ Then what can you do to avoid meeting Him like that?
_____

10. Abraham is an example of faith made perfect by works (21-23).

    a. By what was Abraham justified? _____

    b. When was he justified? _____

    c. With what was his faith "wrought" ("working together" NKJV, or "working" NASB)? _____

    d. How was his faith made perfect? _____

    e. Go back to question three and review the different kinds of works and tell by which kind of works Abraham was justified. _____
    _____

    f. The scripture says, it [Abraham's faith] was imputed unto him for righteousness. To "impute" is to put to his account, to reckon. Was this "by faith only?" Or by a faith that worked the commandments of God? _____

11. Study the apostle Paul's use of Abraham as an example of justification by faith not by works (Rom. 4:1-5, 16-22). James said Abraham was justified "by works" and not by faith only, while Paul said he was justified "by faith" and not by works. It should be apparent that Paul and James are speaking about different kinds of works. Let's see what kind of works were excluded by Paul.

    a. Verse 2 says it was works by which he could glory. Go back to question three: What kind of works would this be? _____

    b. Verse 4 says the works excluded are the works that earn a reward. Would this be meritorious works? _____

    c. Did Abraham obey God before he was justified? _____
    If you answer "No," then go back and read James 2:22 again.

12. Harmonizing the scripture and reaching the conclusion, Paul said Abraham was justified by faith and not by works. James said, Abraham was justified by works and not by faith only. This is not a contradiction. When the contexts are studied it becomes evident that both are teaching the same thing. Paul is excluding meritorious

works of which Abraham could have glorified and received a reward, such works are always excluded, while James is including "works of righteousness" or obedience to God, which are necessary.

a.   What kind of works made Abraham's faith perfect? _____

b.   Those kinds of works are included in justification. Do you agree?____

c.   A conclusion Paul reaches is: Abraham's example of justification by faith was written for us, "to whom it shall be imputed, if we believe on him that raised up Jesus from the dead" (Rom. 4:23-24). If we have the same kind of faith that Abraham had, then "it" (that "kind" of faith) shall be imputed unto us for righteousness. What kind of faith did Abraham have? Was it "faith only" or "faith made perfect by works" of obedience to God? _____

Are we made righteous by faith only? or by faith that obeys God?

_____

d.   A conclusion James reached was: "Ye see then how that by works a man is justified, and not by faith only" (2:24). If we show the same kind of works that Abraham showed, then we will have the same kind of faith that Abraham had.

What kind of works did Abraham show? _____

Could he boast of those works? _____

When we work that "kind" of works in order to be justified before God, can we boast of those works? _____

e.   An application: God commands us to believe in Christ (Mark 16:16), to repent of our sins (Acts 2:38), to confess our faith in Christ before men (Matt. 10:32; Acts 8:37), and be baptized "for the remission of sins" (Acts 2:38). When we do this we are obeying the Lord. We are justified by faith and justified by works, and we are "justified freely by his grace" (Rom. 3:24), for the grace of God made it possible, and we are justified by His blood or the sacrificial death of Jesus (Rom. 5:9).

> When Paul said, "Therefore being justified by faith" (Rom. 5:1), his statement does not exclude "justified ... by his grace" (3:24), "justified by his blood" (5:9), neither does it exclude justified by works (James 2:24).

13. The expression "by faith only" is found but one time in the Bible. What does God say about it (24)? _____

14. Who is the next example of being justified by works (25)? _____

    a. When was she justified? _____

    b. Was she saved by faith (Heb. 11:31)? _____

    c. Can you see that she showed her faith by her works? _____

15. Still on the same subject of faith and works, James uses the example of the body and spirit (26).

    a. What is the condition of the body without the spirit? _____

    b. What is the condition of faith without works? _____
       Can one be saved by that "kind" of faith? _____

16. Read Ecclesiastes 12:13. What is the whole duty of man? _____
    _____

17. Who shall be accepted with God (Acts 10:34-35)? _____
    _____

18. From all of this study can you see that the faith that saves is the faith that causes one to obey the commandments of God? _____

The Epistle of James: Chapter 3

THE UNRULY MEMBER (VS. 1-13)

1. James says, "My brethren, be not many _____." Cf. NASB and NKJV, what word do they use? _____

   a. What shall teachers receive? _____

   b. Is it a serious thing to be a teacher of God's word? _____

   c. Could it be serious to fail to teach the truth that we know? _____

2. Do teachers sometimes offend others? _____

   a. Are some offended by the word of God? _____
      What does offend mean? _____

3. Who is said to be a perfect man? _____

   _____

   What does "perfect" mean? _____
   What is the perfect man able to do? _____

4. What is a bridle? _____

   a. Why is a bit placed in a horse's mouth? _____

   b. With a small bit what is the handler of the horse able to do? ____

   _____

   c. What does it mean to "bridle" the tongue? _____

5. What turns about a ship? _____

   a. With a small helm what is the governor of the ship able to do?

   _____

   b. What lesson is James teaching when he talks about the bit and the helm? _____

    c.   What kind of member is the tongue (5)? _____

6.   What is the tongue called in verse six (two things)? _____

_____

    a.   What is a little fire able to do (6)? _____

    b.   What can the tongue do that would make it a "world of iniquity"?

_____

    What is iniquity? _____

7.   According to James, what has been tamed by man (7)? _____

    a.   What is it that man cannot tame?_____

8.   What two things tell what the tongue is (8)? _____

_____

    a.   Why is the tongue called an unruly evil? _____

    b.   How can a tongue be compared to deadly poison? _____

_____

9.   What are two things we do with our tongues (9-10)? _____

_____

    a.   Is it right to bless God? _____
       Is it right to curse men? _____
       Why not?_____

10.   To show the inconsistency of the same tongue speaking blessings and cursings, James gives three illustrations (11-12). What are they?

    a.   _____

    b.   _____

    c.   _____

    Can you understand each of these illustrations?_____

WISDOM FROM ABOVE VS. WISDOM OF THE EARTH (VS. 13-18)

1.   What kind of man does James refer to in verse 13? _____

     a.   What is the wise man to show? _____

     b.   How does he show his works? (Cf. NKJV) _____

     c.   Can those who hear our words and see our works tell the kind of
          person we are? _____
          How did Jesus say you shall know a man (Matt. 7:20)? _____
          _____

2.   Regarding our words, read Matthew 12:34-37.

     a.   Out of what does the mouth speak? _____

     b.   If you speak evil what does this tell others? _____

     c.   Of what shall we give an account in the day of judgment? _____
          _____

     d.   By your words you shall be _____ or you shall be
          _____. Does this mean that our words will be the only thing
          considered at judgment? _____ Read Revelation 20:13 and 2
          Corinthians 5:10 and tell what we shall give account of that day.
          _____

3.   In verses 14-16 James speaks of envy and strife. Consider the
     following questions:

     a.   What is envy? _____

     b.   What is strife? _____

     c.   Where there is envy and strife what else will be there? _____
          _____

     d.   How are such things described (15)? _____
          _____

What seven things describe the "wisdom that is from above" (17)?

_____

_____

4.   What is said "of them that make peace" (18)? _____

_____

5.   Peace is a most desirable thing, but what has God put before peace?
      _____ Do you think brethren should have "peace at any
      price"?_____ Give the reason for your answer. _____

      _____

The Epistle of James: Chapter 4

PRIDE AND ITS FRUIT (VS. 1-6)

Pride is "of the world" (1 John 2:15-17) and is the cause of the downfall of many. In the N.T. the word translated "pride" is, in other instances, translated "boast," "vainglory," "haughty," and "high-minded," which should tell us something of the nature of pride. It is often the underlying cause of other sins.

1.   Why do men have wars? "Where do wars and fights come from among you" (1, NKJV)? _____

   a.   Are not many fights the fruit of vainglory, or boasting?_____

2.   What are three things that men do, according to verse two? _____

   _____

   a.   Why do men not have these things? _____

3.   When men ask, why do they sometimes not receive (3)? _____

   _____

   a.   Does this mean that it is wrong to ask for things that you need (Cf. Matt. 6:11)? _____

GOD OR THE WORLD – PRIDE OR HUMILITY (VS. 4-10)

1.   When speaking of "friendship of the world" what does James call the people (4)? _____

   a.   Does it seem strange that he would call the people of God such things? _____

   b.   Is adultery still a sign of friendship of the world? _____
        Could adultery be associated with pride of life? _____

   c.   What does James call friendship of the world? _____

   _____

What about the one who wants to be a friend of the world; what does he become? _____

Are there still some children of God who are, in reality, enemies of God? _____

Would they always admit to such? _____

d.   What did John tell Christians about the world (1 John 2:15-17)?

_____

2.   What does the Scripture say regarding "the spirit that dwelleth in us?" (5)_____

Note: When a N.T. writer refers to the "Scripture" it is a reference to the O.T., and reference Bibles usually tell us the specific O.T. verse. On this verse there is none. Consider the following comment: "There is no specific passage in the Old Testament which verbally asserts that which James affirms. There are statements which mean much the same thing as his statement, and it is highly probable that the writer refers to one of these, or, indeed, to all of them, in principle. In which case, the meaning would be, 'Do you suppose that the general teaching of the scripture is without significance in this matter?' ...The statement was, by him, doubtless put in question form for emphasis, signifying, 'The scripture does not speak in vain when it declares that the friendship of the world is enmity with God'" (W—214-215).

a.   What does envy ("jealousy" NKJV) mean?_____

_____

3.   Do the Scriptures ever speak in vain? _____

What words did the Lord put in the mouth of Balaam (Num. 23:19)?

_____

_____

a.   Do you think God's word is vain when He says you cannot be a friend of the world without being an enemy of God? _____

4.   What does God say about the proud (6)? _____

_____

5. What does God give unto the humble? _____
    "But the spirit giveth the knowledge of a more gracious method of
    dealing with unbelievers" (M—598).

6. Unto whom should Christians submit (7)? _____

    a. How does one show submission unto God (Cf. Luke 6:46)? _____

    _____

7. How can one get the devil to flee from him (7)? _____

    a. Should there be a "total rejection" of his efforts? _____
        Will the devil seek a compromise? _____

    b. If one resists the devil on a particular occasion will he return
        again (1 Peter 5:8)? _____
        What should one do then? _____

8. What happens when one draws near unto God (8)? _____
    Do you desire this?_____

    a. Get close to God! What were David's words to Solomon? (1 Chron.
        28:9) _____

    b. Read 2 Chronicles 15:2 and answer three questions:

        (1) "The Lord is with you" when? _____

        (2) "He will forsake you" when?_____

        (3) Does this mean that man will choose whether he wants to be
             close to the Lord? _____

9. What are "sinners" charged to do (8)? _____

    _____

    a. How do we "cleanse our hands" (1 Peter 1:22; 2 Cor. 6:17-7:1)?

    _____

    b. What are the double minded to do? _____

    _____

        What is the seat and source of sin (Matt. 15:19-20)? _____

    c.   Read Isaiah 1:6-20 and learn what God demanded of Israel. Was He willing to cleanse them? _____
What were the people to do? _____
_____

10.   Read verse 9 and tell three things James told the children of God to do. _____
_____

    a.   "Afflicted" signifies to be wretched, to carry and be conscious of heavy burden. Should we feel this way over our sins? _____

    b.   What did Jesus pronounce upon those "that laugh now" (Luke 6:25)? _____
What blessing was awaiting those "that mourn" over their sinful state (Matt. 5:4)? _____

    c.   Heaviness is "downcast eyes, sorrowful dejection." How did Jesus describe the sinner who went to the temple to pray? (Luke 18:13)
_____

11.   "Let your laughter be turned to _____,
and your joy to _____."

    a.   Does this mean it is wrong for Christians to laugh? _____
To be joyful? _____
Is this mourning and heaviness an evident sign of sorrow for sins?
_____

        (1) Read Luke 22:55-62. Why did Peter weep? _____
Was he weeping because of his sin? _____

        (2) How did one sinful woman show sorrow for her sins and love for the Lord (Luke 7:37-38, 47-50)? _____
_____

12.   Why do you think our laughter should be "turned to mourning, and [our] joy to heaviness"? _____
Note: Laughter is outward in character while joy is inward. Does this mean the whole man should be sorrowful because of his sins?

a. How did Jesus describe the sinner who went to the temple to pray (Luke 18:13-14)? _____

13. When we humble ourselves in the sight of the Lord, what will he do for us (10)? _____
How do we humble ourselves? _____
_____

14. What should we not speak of one another (11)? _____

a. When we speak evil of one another and judge one another what have we become? (11) _____

b. Does this mean all judging is wrong (See John 7:24)? _____

c. Who did James say would be blessed (See 1:25)? _____

15. Who is the lawgiver (15)? _____
What is the lawgiver able to do? _____

16. What were some saying we will do on tomorrow (13)? _____
_____
Do many still think like this? _____

a. What do you know about tomorrow (14)? _____

b. Unto what is your life compared (14)? _____

c. How should we speak of our plans for tomorrow (15)? _____
_____
Do you do this? _____

17. In what do many folks rejoice (16)? _____
What does God say of this kind of boasting? _____

18. What does James describe as sin (17)? _____
"Sin" literally means "to miss the mark." When one fails to do what he knows God wants him to do, is he "missing the mark"? _____

a. Read 1 John 3:4. What did John say sin is? _____

b. What else does John call sin (1 John 5:17)? _____

The Epistle of James: Chapter 5

ABOUT THE RICH (VS. 1-6)

1. What are the rich men told to do? _____

   _____

   Note: "Though his readers are again and again called 'brethren,'
   (i.e. four times in the six verses from James 5:7), in no instance are
   these so designated...That the statement of the writer is a solemn
   pronouncement of woe, rather than a call to repentance, indicates the
   utter abandonment to the world which was characteristic of them"
   (W—256).

   a. Why should they weep (1)? _____

   b. Does this mean that one who is rich could not please God? _____

2. According to James what shall happen to:

   a. Riches? _____
      Note: "The circumstances show that the apostle is speaking of
      stores of corn, wind and oil" (M), which could corrupt.

   b. Garments? _____

   c. Gold and silver? _____

   Note: Does this indicate that these riches were not being used?_____

3. What was to be a witness against the rich (3)? _____
   What does this mean? _____
   How will it affect them? _____

4. What have the rich heaped up for the last days (3)? _____
   Does this mean it is wrong for one to "save for a rainy day?" _____

5. What did the rich do with the hire of laborers (4)? _____

What did the law of Moses teach regarding the wages of the laborers? (Lev. 19:13) _____

6.   What did these wages that were kept back do (4)? _____
     Who heard the cries of them who reaped? _____
     (Sabaoth is the transliteration of a Hebrew word which denotes hosts or armies.—Vine). Who is "the Lord of Sabaoth"? _____

7.   Read verses 5-6 and list four things the rich men did.

     a.   _____

     b.   _____

     c.   _____

     d.   _____

8.   What did Jesus say about those who have riches (Luke 18:24-25)?

     _____

9.   Read 1 Timothy 6:6-10 and answer the following questions:

     a.   What does God say is great gain? _____

     b.   How much did we bring into this world? _____

     c.   What did God say is "certain?" _____
          Do you believe this? _____ Do some act as if they do not? _____

     d.   We should be content when we have what? _____

     e.   What will come to those who "will be rich"? _____

     f.   What is the root of all kinds of evil (1 Tim. 6:10)? _____

     g.   What of those who covet after money? _____

     h.   Do you think it is dangerous to be rich? _____ Why? _____

          _____

          Is it dangerous to be poor? _____ Explain your answer. _____

          _____

A STUDY OF PATIENCE (VS. 7-11)

Remember, this epistle was written about 62 A.D., just a few years before the siege of Jerusalem. Although Jewish Christians had already undergone great persecution, lying ahead was the greatest tribulation ever to befall a city and a people, when, with no consideration of religious or irreligious, whether rich or poor, millions of Jews were put to death. The people of God would need great patience.

1. Define "patience." _____

   _____

2. Unto what are Christians to be patient (7)? _____
   Note: This could have a double meaning: "James meant his coming to destroy the Jewish commonwealth" (M—601), as well as the final judgment. In view of either, patience is greatly needed.

3. To illustrate the need of patience, James refers to the natural patience of whom (7)? _____

   a. For what does he wait? _____

   b. Why does he patiently wait? _____

   c. For what must we have patience? _____

4. What two things are Christians told to do (8)? _____

   _____

   a. What is taught in Hebrews 10:36? _____

   _____

5. What did James say about "the coming of the Lord"? _____

   _____

   What does this mean? _____
   If James meant the destruction of the Jewish commonwealth, it was very near.

6. What does "grudge" mean? (9) _____

   _____

   (Cf. "grumble" NKJV, "complain" NASB, some translate it "groan")

    a.   What of those who grudge one against another? _____

_____

    b.   Can holding a grudge cause one to lose patience? _____

    c.   When surrounded by tribulations, hardships, difficulties, etc. is it not better for brethren to exercise patience and encourage each other, rather than groan and complain?_____

7.   Who has been appointed to be the judge of all men (Acts 17:31)? _____

    a.   What does the expression "standeth before the door" mean?

_____

8.   The prophets, who have spoken in the name of the Lord, are cited as an example of what two things (10)? _____

_____

    a.   Should this make us want to learn more of those men? _____

    b.   Where do we read to learn more of them? List scripture references. _____

    c.   Read Romans 15:4 and tell why those Old Testament Scriptures were written. _____

9.   What Old Testament man is cited as an example of patience? (11) _____

    a.   After Job endured how did the Lord bless him (See Job 42:12)?

_____

    b.   How do we count them who endure (11)? _____
        Why do we call them happy or blessed? Is it because they did endure? _____ If they had given up, forsaken God and His word, would we still honor them and call them blessed? _____

    c.   Read Hebrews 11:32-38 and tell some of the sufferings of those holy men of old. _____

_____

    d.   "It is the determination to serve God, whatever the odds, plus patient endurance, that prompts succeeding generations to call those who thus endure blessed" (W—284).

10. What is said of the Lord in verse 11? _____

    a. Do you believe this? _____ Should this help you to develop greater patience, endurance?_____

11. "Above all things" what were they not to do? (12) _____

    a. Why not swear? _____

    b. What did Jesus teach about swearing? (Matt. 5:34-37) _____
    _____

    c. What did Jesus say about our words? (Matt. 12: 36-37) _____
    _____

    d. Does swearing often indicate a lack of self-control? _____
    "One is profane who uses sacred things in an irreverent and blasphemous manner. The word vain, in the third commandment of the Decalogue, is translated from a word in the Hebrew language which means a light, flippant and contemptuous fashion. It is of serious consequence that many members of the church today have allowed to creep into their phraseology words and phrases the use of which amounts to profanity. Others, who would not dare use the holy names, God, Christ, Jesus, Jerusalem, Heaven, Hell, Hades, as interjections ('an ejaculatory word or form of speech, usually thrown in without grammatical connection,' *Webster*) and for emphasis, will, nevertheless, use euphemisms (the substitution of a word or phrase less offensive or objectionable), the derivation of which goes back to one of the foregoing forms. Were those who thus do aware of the origin of many of these common by-words they would be shocked! It is therefore important that we obtain a clear conception of the significance of such words and phrases and avoid all which even indirectly border on the profane. Among them are such words as Gee Whiz, Gosh, Gad, Egad, Golly, Good Gracious, Good Grief, My Goodness, Jeminy, Zounds, Jove, etc., etc." (W—290)

While on the subject of euphemisms let's notice a few:

"Gee" is an euphemistic construction of the name of Jesus. It is in effect to say, "Jesus!" (Webster says it is "a minced form of Jesus, used in mild oaths.")

"Gosh" is an interjection and is used euphemistically for God. ("A softened form of God, used as a mild oath", *The Century Dictionary*)

"Gad" and "Egad" are interjections and are used for the word "God" in mild oaths. "Gee," "Gosh," "Gad," "Egad," and similar forms are used synonymously. They are often joined with other terms for further emphasis, such as "Gee Whilikins" and "Gad Bodkins," of which usage the *Unabridged Dictionary* says, "A softened form of the word God as used in a mild oath or mild oaths in which the second element is often a corruption or made up word."

"Golly" is used for God, often in conjunction with the word "by," i.e., "By Golly!" (Ibid. 290-291).

THE SICK AND PRAYERS (VS. 13-18)

Note: To understand some things in these verses the student must be aware of the fact that in the apostolic days there were "spiritual gifts" (See 1 Cor. 12:1, 7-10 for a listing of these gifts.), one of which was "the gift of healing." It is obvious that the elders in this context had this gift of healing; therefore, the sick person was to call the elders and they were to "pray over him, anointing him with oil in the name of the Lord: and the prayer of faith shall save the sick." Notice that such "shall save the sick," not "might save." These gifts were given only by the laying on of the apostles' hands (see Acts 8:13-18; 19:6); therefore, such gifts would cease when the apostles died. Today the prayers of the elders have no special power above the prayers of any faithful Christian, but we are all to "pray one for another, that ye may be healed" (16). There is power in the prayer of the righteous man (1 Peter 3:12).

1. What are the afflicted to do? (13)? _____

    a. Are those not afflicted to pray? _____

2. What are the merry to do? _____

    a. Are those who are not merry to sing? _____
        Note: The writer is instructing those who are "afflicted" and those
        who are "merry." It is special instructions. Those not afflicted and
        those who are not merry are not under consideration. To learn
        their duties and responsibilities one must read where general
        instruction is given.

3. "Is any sick among you?" If so, what was he to do?_____

    a. What were the elders to do for the sick (14)? _____
        "Send for the elders of the church—namely where the sick person
        lives...In the first age the spiritual gifts were dispersed in such
        plenty, that no church was without these gifts; and particularly,
        in every church there were some who possessed the gift of
        miraculously healing the sick" (M—602).

    b. "Anointing him with oil in the name of the Lord." When the
        disciples were sent to preach to the house of Israel, they were
        given power to heal the sick (See Matt. 10:8). When Mark writes of
        their doing this, what does he say (Mark 6:13)? _____
        _____
        "The anointing the sick with oil was not prescribed, either by our
        Lord or by his apostles, as a natural remedy, but as a sensible
        token to the sick person himself, and to those who were present,
        that a miracle of healing was going to be performed. Where no
        miracle is to be performed, to use anointing, as a religious rite, is
        a vain superstition" (M—602).

4. What two things shall be the result of the prayers of elders for the sick
    (15)? _____

5. Are others, besides the elders, to pray for the healing of one another
    (16)? _____

6.   What kind of prayer "availeth much" (16)? _____

_____

7.   To further illustrate the power of prayer, James refers to one of the prophets. To whom? _____
What kind of man was he? _____

a.   For what did Elijah pray? _____

b.   Why did Elijah ask such a thing (1 Kings 17-18)? _____

_____

c.   Is James telling his brethren that prayer can accomplish things?

_____

d.   Read 1 Peter 3:12. What did Peter say about God and the prayers of His people? _____

_____

8.   What has James already said about our prayers?
a. (1:6) _____
b. (4:3) _____

RESTORING THE ERRING (VS. 19-20)

1.   What is the truth (See John 1:17; 17:17; 1 Peter 1:22, 25)? _____

_____

2.   What does it mean to "err" from the truth? _____
Compare NASB and NKJV _____

3.   What does "convert" mean? _____

4.   What did Jesus teach about being converted (Matt. 18:3)? _____

_____

5.   James is writing to those who were in the kingdom. Had they been converted? Think! _____ Can one who has been converted later sin and need to be converted again? Think! _____

6.   What happens when one who has erred from the truth is converted?

_____

    a. From what death does he save a soul (Rev. 20:15)? _____

    b. How does he hide a multitude of sins? _____

    _____

7.   Read Acts 8:13-24 to see an example of this.

    a. Was Simon the sorcerer converted? _____

    b. Later, how did he err from the truth (18-19)? _____

    _____

    c. What did Peter say Simon had thought? _____

    _____

    d. How did Peter describe Simon's condition (21)? _____

    e. What did Peter tell him to do (22)? _____

    f. What did Simon do (24)? _____

    g. Today, when one errs from the truth, must he do what Simon did?

    _____

8.   Compare Paul's instructions in Galatians 6:1 to these verses.

    a. How did Paul speak of the man who erred? _____

    _____

    b. Who is to restore such an one? _____

    c. When we try to restore one who is overtaken in a fault or convert one who has erred, what must we consider? _____

    d. Why must we consider ourselves?_____

9.   Give your personal opinion: Is seeking to convert one who has erred from the truth or to restore one who has been overtaken in a fault a worthwhile thing to do?_____

The First Epistle of Peter: Chapter 1

This epistle was written about 63 to 67 A.D. when persecution was common and the temptation to turn from Christ was great. It was written for the purpose of "exhorting, and testifying that this is the true grace of God wherein ye stand" (5:12). It is a general letter to the disciples of Christ of Peter's generation, with many lessons applying to every generation of the disciples.

"Simon was a native of Bethsaida, a town situated on the western shore of the lake of Gennesareth. He was by trade a fisherman, and had a brother, Andrew ... Their father was named Jonah or John; and probably was of the same occupation with his sons. Andrew was a disciple of John the Baptist (John 1:35, 41) and he heard him point out Jesus as 'the Lamb of God which taketh away the sin of the world.' This good news Andrew communicated to his brother Simon, and brought him to Jesus; who, foreseeing the fortitude he would exercise in preaching the gospel, honored him with the name of Cephas or Peter, which is by interpretation a stone or rock, John 1:42" (M—603).

As to the design in writing this epistle, "To comfort and encourage their suffering brethren ... he represented to them the obligations the disciples of Christ were under to suffer for their religion; and suggested a variety of motives to persuade them to suffer cheerfully ... though this epistle had an especial reference to the circumstance of the Christians in the first age, it is still of great use for enforcing the obligations of morality and in promoting holiness among the professors of the gospel" (Ibid—607).

THE GREETING (VS. 1-2)

1. How did Peter identify himself? _____

   _____

   The role of the apostles of Christ may be seen in several passages (The word "apostle" means "one sent."):

   a. In Acts 1:8 they are called _____

   _____

  b.   In 2 Corinthians 5:20 they are the _____
       of Christ, unto whom the Spirit revealed the truth (An
       ambassador is an official representative of another.).

  c.   Questions about the revelation of truth:

       (1) What part of truth was to be made known to them (Jn. 16:13)?
            _____

       (2) Who revealed the truth to them (1 Cor. 2:10)? _____

       (3) In whose words did they speak this truth (1 Cor. 2:13)? _____

       (4) Paul was not among that number, but became an apostle
            later. How did he receive the truth (Gal. 1:12, 16)? _____
            _____

       (5) Is it possible for us to know this same truth (Eph. 3: 3-4)? _____

  d.   Questions about apostles:

       (1) Are there men today who are eye witnesses of Christ? _____

       (2) Are there men today who are ambassadors of Christ? _____

       (3) Are there men today to whom the Spirit is revealing truth? _____

       (4) Then are there any apostles of Christ living among us? _____

2.   To whom was the letter addressed? _____
     _____

  a.   Why were they scattered? (Acts 8:1, although many years earlier,
       may give a clue.) _____

3.   What are these people called? _____

  a.   What is another word for "elect" (Cf. NASB)? _____

  b.   Who had chosen them? _____

  c.   Their election was "according to" what? _____
       What is "foreknowledge"? _____
       _____

d. Their election was "through" ("in" NKJV, "by" NASB) what? _____

_____

Compare to 2 Thess. 2:13-14. _____

e. They were elect, or chosen, unto what? _____

f. Is "sprinkling of the blood" connected with obedience? _____

g. When does the blood of Christ (the benefit of the sacrifice of Christ) wash away the sins of believers (See Acts 22:16; Romans 6:3-4)? _____

4. What did Peter desire to be multiplied unto them?_____

THE INHERITANCE (VS. 3-12)

1. Unto what has God begotten us? _____
   What does the NASB say in place of "begotten"? _____

2. Peter says our being begotten (born again) is "according to _____."

3. We have this living hope through or by the "_____ of _____ _____ from the _____."

   a. How did Paul refer to Christ and His resurrection from the dead, in 1 Cor. 15:20? _____

   _____

4. In verse four what does Peter call this living hope? _____

5. What four terms describe this inheritance? Tell what each one means.

   a. _____

   b. _____

   c. _____

   d. _____

6. How are God's people kept? _____

   a. How does faith come (Rom. 10:17)? _____

   _____

    b.   How can faith keep us or guard or protect us? _____

_____

7.   Unto what are we being kept? _____

    a.   Is this salvation the same as the inheritance of verse 4?_____

8.   In what do God's people greatly rejoice? _____

9.   In what were they "in heaviness" ("grieved" NKJV, "distressed" NASB)?

_____

10.   What is "more precious than gold"? _____
Question: Is your faith more precious to you than gold? _____
As this is being written, gold is worth nearly five hundred dollars an ounce.
Yet, every ounce of gold will one day perish. What about your faith?

11.   Disciples should live so that at the appearing of Jesus their faith might
be found unto what?_____

    a.   Is this the same as being faithful, even unto death (Rev. 2:10)? _____

12.   Whom did they love even though they had not seen him?_____

    a.   Do you love this Christ?   _____

    b.   In whom did they believe although they had not seen him? _____

    c.   What did Christ say about such persons (John 20:29)? _____

    d.   Are you among those blessed ones? _____

13.   Why did they "rejoice with joy unspeakable"? THINK! _____

_____

14.   What were they to receive in "the end of your faith"? _____

    a.   Is this the same as the inheritance of verse 4? _____

    b.   What does "the end of your faith" mean?_____
(The end does not always mean the termination of a thing, but
may be that to which it directs. Paul said, "Christ is the end of the
law for righteousness" (Rom. 10:4) that to which the law directed
the Jews.)

15. Regarding this salvation, what had the prophets done?_____
_____

   a. What had they prophesied? _____

   b. What Spirit was in those prophets? _____
       What does Ephesians 4:4 tell us of the Spirit? _____
       _____

   c. What was revealed unto those prophets? _____
       _____

   d. What did Paul say of those things that are "revealed ... unto us
       [apostles]" (1 Cor. 2:1-10)? _____
       _____

       Note: When Isaiah the prophet wrote those words (Isa. 64:4),
       even the prophets had not seen or heard all the things God had
       planned for His people. We now know these things because they
       were revealed to the apostles.

   e. These "things which are now reported unto you by them that
       have" what (12)? _____

LIVING BEFORE GOD WHO REDEEMED US (VS. 13-21)

1. What are God's people charged to do? _____
_____

   a. Is the grace that is to be brought unto them the same as the
       inheritance of verse four? _____

   b. When is this grace to be brought (13)? _____

2. What kind of children were the elect to be (14)? _____

   a. They were not to fashion themselves according to what? _____
       _____

3. As the Lord is holy God's children must be holy in what? _____

4. What does Peter say with reference to the Father (17)? _____
_____

5. If we recognize the Father and call upon him as Father, how should we conduct ourselves throughout life (17)? _____

    a. What did the wise man say about the fear of the Lord (Prov. 1:7)?
        _____

    b. What did Peter say about fearing God (Acts 10:35)? _____
        _____

    c. Do you have this fear (reverence) of God?_____

6. Peter wrote of the negative and positive aspects of our redemption (18-19).

    a. We are not redeemed with _____ .

    b. We are redeemed with _____ .

    c. From what were they redeemed (18)? _____

7. How is Christ referred to in verse 19? _____

    a. How had John introduced him unto his disciples (John 1:29)? ___
        _____

    b. Why was He called a lamb? _____

    c. When did God foreordain that redemption would be by the blood of Christ (20)?_____

8. Now do some thinking about "the blood of Christ."

    a. Read Hebrews 10:10 and tell by what offering we are sanctified.
        _____

    b. How did Christ "put away sin" (Heb. 9:26)? _____
        _____

    c. Now read Hebrews 9:15 and tell how redemption was made possible. _____

    d. Conclusion: Is "the death of Jesus" the same as the "offering of the body of Jesus"? _____ Is the "offering of the body" the same as "the sacrifice of himself"? _____ Is the "sacrifice of himself" the same as the shedding of "the blood"? _____ Then, is "the blood of Christ" just another way of saying "sacrifice"? _____ When Peter said you were redeemed "with the precious blood of Christ," is he talking about the "bloodiness" [the blood shed when the Roman solider pierced his side with the spear (John 19:34)], or the "sacrifice" of Christ, that had already been made? _____

9. Who raised Jesus from the dead (21)?_____

   a. When He raised Him up from the dead, what did He give Him (21)?
   _____

   What does this mean (Eph. 1:21-22)? _____
   _____

10. God raised Jesus from the dead "so that" what (21)? _____
   _____

   a. Does the faith of men sometimes stand in something other than in God? _____ Read 1 Corinthians 2:5 and tell in what the faith of some stands? _____

   b. Does the hope of men often stand in the wisdom of men? _____

   c. What does Paul say about the hope (Eph. 4:4)? _____
   _____

   d. What is the "one hope" of the gospel (See Titus 1:2; 2 Tim. 4:8)?
   _____

THE ENDURING WORD (VS. 22-25)

1. How do we purify our souls? _____
   _____

   a. Is obeying the same as believing? THINK! _____

   b. Which comes first: believing or obeying? THINK! _____

   c. Does this sound like salvation by faith only? _____

   d. What was involved in obeying the truth? Whatever was involved it was necessary to purifying the soul. Since those of Galatia are addressed in this letter (1:1), to learn what they did is to learn what is involved. Read Galatians 3:26-27 and tell what they did.

_____

Then this must be necessary for purifying the soul. Do you agree?

_____

What did Ananias say would occur when the believer (Saul) was baptized (Acts 22:16)? _____

Is this the same as "purifying the soul"? _____

Is this what Jesus said one must do to be saved? (Mark 16:16) _____

2. What are those who have purified their souls charged to do (22)?

_____

3. Peter refers to this purifying of the soul as "being born again."

a. What had Jesus taught about the importance of being born again (John 3:3-5)? _____

b. Since we know how they purified their souls, do we know how they were born again? THINK! _____

c. What seed produces this birth (23)? _____

What did Jesus say the "seed" is (Luke 8:11)? _____

d. What two things are said of the word of God (23)? _____

_____

4. To what is all flesh compared? _____

And all the glory of men? _____

a. What happens to the grass? _____

What is this saying about all flesh? _____

b. What happens to the flower? _____

What is this teaching about the glory of men? _____

c. With this in view, should we put our trust in other men? _____

Or our hope in the glory of men? _____

5. "The word of the Lord endureth _____."

a.   What is another term for the word of the Lord (25)? _____

b.   What did Jesus say about His words (Matt. 24:35)? _____

_____

c.   Read Psalm 19:7-11. How much should we desire the word of
      God? _____
      How sweet should it be to us? _____

The First Epistle of Peter: Chapter 2

DESIRE THE WORD (VS. 1-3)

1. "Wherefore," in verse one, indicates in view of a conclusion just reached. What was the conclusion? _____
"Seeing ye are born again through the incorruptible seed of the word" (M).

2. Read the sentence in its entirety (1-3) and reconstruct it beginning with verse 3: "If so be ye have tasted that the Lord is gracious, wherefore ("therefore" NKJV), laying aside all malice and all guile."

   a. In our English the word "if" means "maybe so, maybe not, or it could be or could not be." And so the word is used many times in the N.T., but not always. Sometimes they used the word "if" to state a matter of certainty (See Col. 3:1 and 1 Cor. 15:12 as examples.). In this text, "If so be ye have tasted that the Lord is gracious," is a matter of certainty. Surely they had already tasted that, so "Because indeed ye have tasted" is the rendering MacKnight gives.

      Question: Is the "ye have tasted" the same thing as "being born again" (1:23) in the conclusion just reached? _____

   b. Since they had been born again by the word of God, "Ye have tasted that the Lord is gracious," what were they to lay aside? List five things and give the meaning of each.

      (1) _____

      (2) _____

      (3) _____

      (4) _____

      (5) _____

    c.   Having been born again, or purified their souls, they were charged to "love one another with a pure heart fervently" (1:22). Do these five things work against such love or promote it? _____

3.   What were they to desire? _____

    a.   What figure is used to emphasize this desire? _____

    b.   What do newborn babes naturally desire? _____

    c.   What should a new Christian desire? _____

    d.   Is Peter saying they were all "newborn babes" in Christ? _____

    e.   What would result from such a desire? _____

    f.   When one has no desire to learn more of the word can we force him to learn? _____ What can we do? _____

CHRIST, THE STONE – CHRISTIANS, LIVING STONES (VS. 4-10)

1.   The figure of the building is in verses 4-8. Under this figure, what is the Lord called? _____

    a.   Living is in contrast to what? _____

    b.   How do men treat this living stone? _____ How was He treated by God? _____

    c.   What other word is used to describe Christ (4)? _____

2.   In this figure what are the disciples called? _____

    a.   What do these living stones build up? _____
    Note: This spiritual house is a contrast to the temple of the Old Testament and to the temples of the pagans.

    b.   Every building is built for a purpose. What was the purpose of the tabernacle and temple under the law? _____
    _____

        (1) What is the purpose of this spiritual house? _____
        _____

(2) What are spiritual sacrifices (Cf. Rom. 12:1)? _____

_____

(3) All sacrifices and service must be acceptable to whom? _____

(4) How can we know a religious service is acceptable to God? THINK! Is it because we like it? _____ Because some board of men like it? _____ Because God has said so? _____

c. What kind of priesthood do the disciples of Christ comprise?

_____

(1) Does this mean each Christian is a priest? _____

(2) Who is the High Priest (Heb. 4:14)? _____

(3) Must we confess our sins to a priest, who in turn prays for us? _____ Since each Christian is a priest, can he go to God through the High Priest?_____

3. Peter quotes from Isaiah 28:16, a prophecy regarding the foundation stone that was to be laid in Zion (Jerusalem). What did Isaiah say about that stone? _____

_____

a. How was Jesus a tried stone? _____

b. How is He a precious stone? _____

c. In what sense is He a cornerstone? The corner has to do with joining two sides together. Who are the two (See Eph. 2:15-22)?

_____

Note, "A principle corner-stone in the foundation, for uniting the two sides of the building. This, as explained in Eph. 2:21, signifies the union of Jews and Gentiles in one faith, baptism, and hope, so as to form one church or temple for the worship of God, through the mediation of Jesus Christ." (M—614).

d. What makes him a sure foundation? _____

_____

4.   What is said about "he that believeth on him"? _____

_____

   a.   What does this mean? (Compare NASB and NKJV) _____

   _____

5.   To whom is Christ precious? _____

   Is he precious to you? _____

6.   What is He "unto them which be disobedient"? _____

   a.   Although Christ is the Savior, will He save those who refuse to
         believe? _____ Or, refuse to obey? _____

   b.   Does "whereunto also they were appointed" mean some had
         no opportunity for salvation? _____ Or, is it that God, in His
         infinite wisdom, ordained that those who disbelieve will stumble
         at the word and be disobedient? _____

7.   The people of God are called four different things in verse 9. Name
      them and be prepared to discuss each term. _____

   _____

   a.   What did Jesus say about the chosen (Matt. 20:16)? _____

   _____

   How were they chosen (See 2 Thess. 2:13)? _____

   _____

   b.   "Royal" is used in reference to kings. Do Christians have a
         relationship with a king? _____ Which king? _____

   c.   The unbelieving Jews were no longer a nation of God, but the
         believers became a holy nation. What makes them holy? _____

   _____

   d.   What kind of people are they? _____
         How does the NASB read? _____

8.   I prefer the NKJV which has it, "His own special people," for I do
      believe Christians are a special people of God, and we should think of
      ourselves as such. Do you agree? _____ As "His own special people,"

we also have special responsibilities. What are some of these? _____

_____

_____

Along with this special relationship we have with God, there are also some special blessings. What are some? _____

_____

9. Out of what had these special people been called? _____
   Where were they as a result of this calling? _____

10. From verse 10, tell what they were not _____
    and what they are now. _____
    that which they "had not obtained" _____
    but have now obtained _____

HOW GOD'S PEOPLE SHOULD LIVE BEFORE THE WORLD (VS. 11-12)

1. How were God's people to act and think regarding fleshly lusts? ____

   _____

   Compare 1 Thess. 5:22. What is commanded there? _____

   _____

2. What do fleshly lusts do? _____

   a. Who will help God's people overcome these lusts (1 Cor. 10:10-12)?

      _____

3. What exhortation is given in verse 12? _____

   _____

   a. What does conversation mean? (See NASB) _____

      _____

   b. Why is it important that the behavior of Christians be always honest? _____

      _____

   c. What is the day of visitation? _____

      _____

CHRISTIANS AND CIVIL RULERS (VS. 13-17)

1. Christians are "an holy nation" unto God, but they live under civil rule in this world. What should be their attitude toward civil rulers? _____

    _____

2. In civil rule kings rank _____
    (13), and they send governors for what purpose? _____

3. Did Paul say the same thing to those at Rome (Rom. 13:1-7)? _____

4. How do Christians put to silence the ignorance of foolish men? _____

    _____

5. Although God's people are free, they have responsibilities. What charge is given regarding this freedom? _____
    See also NASB _____

6. What four charges are found in verse seventeen? _____

    _____

    a. Do these affect the Christian's influence in this world? _____

    b. What did the wise man say about the fear of God? (Prov. 1:7) _____

        _____

    c. Does "honor the king" mean that we should honor our president?

        _____

SERVANTS AND MASTERS (VS. 18-25)

1. What is the charge to servants? _____

2. What kind of masters are mentioned in verse 18? _____

    a. What does "forward" mean? _____

    b. Compare the NASB, what word is used? _____

    c. How does the NKJV read? _____

3. What did Peter say is "thankworthy" or "commendable" (NKJV)? _____

    _____

a. Were many Christians then suffering wrongfully? _____

4. If a Christian suffers because of some wrong or foolish thing he has done, is there any glory in that? _____
What if he suffers when he has done no wrong, how is he before God? _____

5. For what purpose were the people of God called? _____

   a. Who left an example for all Christians? _____

6. Name four things Christ did in leaving us an example.

   a. _____

   b. _____

   c. _____

   d. _____

7. How did Jesus "bear our sins"? _____

   a. Does this show the greatest degree of obedience to God? _____

   b. Should we follow this example of obedience? _____

8. What does it mean "that we, being dead to sins" (24)? _____
   _____
   See NASB _____

9. What was made possible by the stripes of Jesus? _____
   _____

   a. Is this the healing of the physical body? Or the healing of the spirit?
      _____

      Note: Jesus healed the bodies of men by miracles and such did not require His death.

10. Before becoming the people of God, how were these people described? _____

11. Who is the Shepherd and Bishop of your soul?_____

The First Epistle of Peter: Chapter 3

INSTRUCTIONS TO WIVES (VS. 1-6)

1.   What does the term "likewise," or "in the same way" (NASB) mean?

     _____

2.   Unto whom are wives to be in subjection? _____

3.   Does verse one necessarily infer that God recognizes the marriage where one is a Christian and the other is not? _____

4.   What is "the word" in the phrase, "obey not the word"? THINK!_____

5.   Can a husband be converted without hearing the word of God? THINK!_____

     a.   If you answered "yes," then read Matthew 28:19 and John 6:44-45. Did Jesus say that all must be taught the word? _____

     b.   Compare the NASB and the NKJV both of which read that the husband may be won "without a word." The husband must "obey the word" but he may be won "without a word." How may he be won? _____

     c.   Peter said, he may be won. What does "won" mean? _____
          Does this necessarily infer that he is lost? _____
          Unto what are all of those who are won to Christ added? (Acts 2:47) _____

6.   What kind of "conversation" or "conduct" (NKJV) should the husband observe in the life of his wife? _____
     With what is such conduct to be coupled or accompanied? _____

     _____

7.   The adorning of the wife is discussed in verses 3-4. Note that it is approached first from the negative, "let it not be," then from the

positive, "but let it be." List the three things it should not be.

_____

   a. Is he saying the woman should not braid her hair? _____
That she should not wear any gold? _____
If so, he is saying she should not wear apparel. Do you agree? _____
Since that cannot be the proper interpretation of the passage,
what does it mean?_____

8.   Now the positive side: "But let it be" what? _____

   a. What is "the hidden man of the heart" called in 2 Cor. 4:16? _____

_____

   b. What is he called in Colossians 3:10? _____

   c. How would you define a "meek and quiet" spirit? _____

_____

   d. How is a "meek and quiet" spirit valued by God?_____

9.   Which women are cited as an example of this kind of adornment?

_____

   a. In whom did such women trust? _____

   b. Unto whom were they in subjection?_____

10.   What woman in particular is named as an example?_____

   a. What do those women who follow her example become?_____

_____

   b. They are her daughters as long as what? _____

_____

   c. The wife is to have proper respect for her husband, but she
should not be afraid of him. "The wife must not obey her husband
because she is 'scared' or frightened into it, but should do it from
a motive of modesty and respect." (Z—259). Do some men try to
scare their wives into subjection?_____

INSTRUCTIONS TO HUSBANDS (V. 7)

1. Husbands are to dwell with their wives according to _____
   "'Dwell', translated from a term which denotes domestic association,
   sums up the relationships of the marriage state." (W—92).

   a. Is a believer permitted to put away a wife, or husband, because
      he or she is not a believer? (1 Cor. 7:12-13) _____

   b. Of what should the husband have knowledge? _____
      Compare to the NASB; what word is used? _____

2. The husband is charged to give "_____
   unto the wife."

3. In what way is the wife the "weaker vessel"? _____

4. In becoming children of God is there any difference in what women
   do and what men do? _____ Read Galatians 3:26-29. What did Paul say
   about male and female becoming children of God? _____

5. As children of God, what do husbands and wives share? _____
   _____

6. What would cause the prayers to be hindered? _____
   _____

   a. Does this necessarily infer that husbands and wives pray? _____

7. If their relationship in marriage is strained by arguing, fighting,
   bitterness, etc., are they as apt to be praying?_____

INSTRUCTIONS TO CHRISTIANS (VS. 8-12)

1. These charges are given to whom? _____

2. What five things are charged in verse 8? _____
   _____
   _____

3. What two things are they told not to do? _____
   _____

4.   Instead of returning evil for evil, what should Christians do? _____

_____

Must we do this to please God? _____

5.   Read Romans 12:14-17. Is the instruction given to the saints at Rome about the same as that which Peter gives? _____

6.   For what purpose were they called? _____
What is that blessing? _____

7.   Five things are charged of "he that will love life, and see good days."
What are they? _____

_____

_____

8.   What does "refrain" mean? _____

9.   What does "eschew" mean? _____

10.   What is said about the eyes of the Lord and the righteous? _____

_____

  a.   Does this mean that the Lord does not see what the unrighteous do? _____ Read Hebrews 4:13 and tell what things are open unto the eyes of the Lord? _____

  b.   Does "the eyes of the Lord are over the righteous" indicate a special care for them? _____

  c.   Read Isaiah 66:2 and tell to whom the Lord will look._____

_____

11.   What is said about the ears of the Lord and the righteous?_____

_____

  a.   Read Isaiah 59:1-2 and tell what will keep the Lord from hearing prayers. _____

  b.   Read Proverbs 28:9 and tell what happens when one turns away his ear from hearing the law. _____

_____

    c.   In view of this, does being righteous give one an advantage with God? _____

12.   What is said about them who do evil? _____

_____

What does that expression mean? _____

_____

SUFFERING FOR RIGHT AND WRONG (VS. 13-17)

1.   Do people generally harm one who does good? _____
Have there been exceptions to this general rule when those who did good were harmed? _____
Who is the greatest example of this (Acts 10:38-39)? _____

2.   What is said about one who suffers for righteousness' sake? _____

_____

Compare Matthew 5:10. _____

_____

3.   Of what should Christians not be afraid? _____

4.   What did Jesus teach about fearing men (Matt. 10:28)? _____

_____

5.   What about one who would lose his life for Christ's sake (Matt. 16:25)?

_____

6.   What does "sanctify" mean? _____

    a.   Who is to be sanctified in the heart of a Christian? _____

    b.   What does this mean?_____

7.   What should Christians be ready to do? _____

    a.   How should the answer be given? _____

8.   What should a Christian always have? _____
Does having a good conscience guarantee acceptability with God?
_____ Give an example. _____

9.   What would make those ashamed who falsely accuse a Christian?

      _____

10.   Regarding suffering, read verse seventeen and tell what is better.

      _____

      What was the prayer of Stephen as unbelievers were stoning him (See
      Acts 7:60)? _____
      In your judgment is it more difficult to suffer for well-doing than to
      suffer for wrong doing? _____

THE SUFFERING OF CHRIST (VS. 18-22)

1.   For what did Christ suffer? _____
      Does suffering, in this reference, mean death? _____

2.   How many sacrifices did He make for sin? _____
      Read Hebrews 9:24-28 and tell how His sacrifice differed from those
      offered before him. _____

3.   For whom did He suffer? _____

4.   Who is the "just" of verse eighteen? _____
      Who are the unjust? _____

5.   He suffered that He might do what? _____
      What separated man from God (Isa. 59:1-2)? _____

6.   What part of Jesus was put to death? _____

7.   Was the spirit of Christ put to death? _____
      Did Jesus show that death is not the end of existence? _____
      Note: Death is a separation. On the cross Jesus cried out with a
      loud voice, "My God, my God, why hast thou forsaken me?" (Matt.
      27:46). Many think this was the most agonizing part of His death, the
      separation from the Father. Many have faced physical death without
      a cry, and our Lord was as strong as they. But to think of separation
      from the Father ... that brought the greatest anguish. Most men have
      this in reverse: They agonize over physical death but think nothing of
      being separated from the Father.

8. "By which [Spirit] He went and preached unto" whom? _____
_____

Note: These spirits were "in prison" because they were disobedient to God, thus were held captive by sin and wickedness. Peter does not say when this preaching was done, but, when considering all that is said of the incident, we conclude that the preaching was done "when once the long suffering of God waited in the days of Noah."

a. What spirit was with the prophets of the Old Testament (1 Peter 1:10-11)? _____

b. The same Spirit was with Noah that was with all the holy men of God. Which Spirit was it (2 Peter 1:21)? _____

9. These spirits were disobedient in the days of whom? _____

10. What did God say regarding His spirit and these men (See Genesis 6:3)? _____

11. Who was the "preacher of righteousness" in those days (2 Peter 2:5)?
_____

12. What did Noah's preaching and action do to the world (Heb. 11:7)?
_____

13. How were those eight souls saved in Noah's time? _____

14. Read Hebrews 11:7. How did Noah save his house? _____
Was it by faith only? _____ What did he do by faith? _____

15. Read Genesis 6:8 and tell what Noah found? _____
What does "grace" mean? _____

16. When we get all that has been said about Noah and his salvation, we will see that he was saved

a. By _____ (2 Peter 2:4-5)

b. By _____ (Genesis 6:8)

c. By _____ (Hebrews 11:7)

d. By _____ (1 Peter 3:20)

17.   Noah's salvation by water is a figure of what? _____

18.   Peter did not say water saves us, but said, " _____
doth also now save us" (Compare NASB and NKJV.).
Note: Our being saved by baptism does not mean we are saved by
baptism only, not any more than Noah's salvation by water meant he
was saved by "water only." We have learned that Noah was saved by
God, by grace, by faith, and by water. Even so we are saved by God, by
grace, by faith, and by baptism.

19.   Does baptism put away the filth of the flesh? _____
If not, what does it do (See Acts 22:16)? _____

20.   What is conscience (See 1 John 3:30-21; Acts 2:27)? _____

_____

21.   Read Mark 16:16. Can one who learns what Jesus has commanded
answer a good conscience without doing what He commanded? _____

22.   Read verse 21 omitting the statement in parenthesis. Would baptism
save us if Jesus had not been raised from the dead? _____
Romans 4:25 says, He was "raised for our _____."

23.   Where has Jesus gone? _____

24.   What position is now His? (See also Matt. 28:18; Eph. 1:20-22)

_____

25.   Who is subject unto the authority of Christ?_____

The First Epistle of Peter: Chapter 4

SUFFERING OF CHRIST, CONTINUED (VS. 1-6)

1. Read verse one. Do you see that the subject is the suffering of Christ which was introduced in 3:18? _____

2. Knowing that Christ has suffered for us, Peter said, "arm yourselves ... with" what? _____
   Read Phil. 2:5. What does Paul say? _____
   Did Christ have the mind of obedience to the Father even to suffering for well-doing? _____ Should Christians have this mind? _____

3. "He that hath suffered in the flesh" is referring to the Christian who has the mind of Christ and is willing to follow His example. What is said of that Christian? _____
   _____
   _____

4. The rest of the sentence (2) tells how that person who has ceased from sin should live. Tell what he should no longer do _____
   and what he should do _____

5. Read Romans 6:2, 7. What did Paul say about the disciple of Christ and sin? _____

6. How had those disciples walked in times past? List things they had done. "The first three sins ... are primarily personal sins; the last three are social evils, and all common to the unregenerate world of the first century" (W—109). _____
   _____
   Does this sound as though they had lived after the flesh? _____
   Are there many who still live like that? _____ Are there some in the church who live like that? _____

7.   What do those of the world think about Christians who once walked with them, but who now refuse to do those things? _____

_____

Note: "The words 'run not with them into the same excess of riot' are significant and impressive. 'Run' denotes more than mere association; it indicates eagerness of participation and fellowship in the vices mentioned. 'Excess' is from a term which means, literally, an overflowing, and in classical Greek referred to gutters suddenly swollen from rains which poured their contents into common sewers" (W—109).

8.   To whom shall all such persons give account? _____
     What does this mean? _____

9.   To whom was the gospel preached? _____
     Read Ephesians 2:1 and tell in what sense they were dead. _____

10.   Why was the gospel preached to them? _____

_____

     Should the gospel still be preached to those who are dead in sins?

_____

SERVING TO GLORIFY GOD (VS. 7-11)

1.   What does "at hand" mean? _____
     What did John preach about the kingdom (Matt. 3:1-2)? _____
     How did Paul describe the time of his departure (2 Tim. 4:6)? _____

2.   To what does the statement "the end of all things" refer? _____

_____

     Is its meaning stated in the text? _____
     Something to think about. Here are some ideas of what it means.

     a.   The destruction of Jerusalem, which was then near and would mark the end of the temple, the end of the Levitical priesthood, and the end of the whole Jewish economy

     b.   If these words could be taken in a general sense then we might say to every present generation, the end of all the good which the wicked enjoy, and the end of the evil which the righteous suffer.

    c.   End of all things is at hand or near, comparatively speaking, for "our life on earth is but a span."

    d.   Some have suggested that it is the end of this world and the judgment. However, since this has been written, more than 1900 years have passed, so that could hardly have been "at hand" when Peter wrote.

3.   What were they to do since "the end of all things [was] at hand"? _____

_____

4.   Above all things what were they to have? _____
"Fervent" is from a word which means "to stretch out, as of a string drawn taut on an instrument ... suggests the intensity which should characterize Christians in their love for one another" (W—112).

5.   What will charity, or love, do? _____
Does this mean if we love someone we will overlook their sins? _____
What does Proverbs 10:12 say? _____

6.   What should Christians use one to another? _____

7.   Hospitality is to be extended without what? _____
One should not show hospitality because he "has to do it," but out of love. Do you agree? _____

8.   What are Christians called in verse ten? _____
What is a steward? _____
How could this apply to using hospitality? _____

9.   If any one speaks, let him speak how? _____

10.   If any one ministers, how should he do it? _____

11.   Whether we speak or minister who should be glorified? _____
Read 1 Corinthians 6:20. How are we to glorify God? _____
Read Ephesians 3:21. In what are we to glorify God? _____
Is "in" referring to place or relationship? _____
Read 1 Corinthians 10:31. What should Christians do to the glory of God? _____

SUFFERING TO THE GLORY OF GOD (VS. 12-19)

1.   What should Christians think to be not strange? _____
       _____

       Why should this not be thought of as a strange thing? _____

       _____

2.   What kind of trial does Peter call it? _____

3.   When tried, why should Christians rejoice? _____

       _____

4.   If we suffer for well-doing, as Christ suffered, how will we be when His
       glory shall be revealed? _____

5.   What does "when his glory shall be revealed" refer to? _____

       _____

6.   "To be reproached" means to be reviled, or have belittling things said
       about you. When Christians are reproached for the name of Christ
       how should they feel? _____
       What does "the name of Christ" mean in this passage? _____

       _____

7.   To endure such reproach shows the spirit that is within one. What
       kind of spirit is it? _____

8.   How do those of the world speak of God? _____
       How do Christians speak of him? _____

9.   List the four things for which Christians are not to suffer and tell what
       each means.

       a.   _____

       b.   _____

       c.   _____

       d.   _____

10.   If any man suffers as a Christian, what should he do? _____

What should he not be? _____

What does this mean? _____

11.   What does it mean to suffer as a Christian? _____
      _____

12.   Verses 17-18 refer to a judgment, but evidently not to the final
      judgment, for at least two reasons. (1) That judgment was coming
      when the letter was written over 1900 years ago (The NASB reads,
      "for it is time for judgment to begin," and the NKJV reads, "For the
      time has come for judgment to begin."). (2) If the righteous one shall
      "scarcely" be saved, but in the final judgment they shall have an
      entrance into the heavenly kingdom abundantly supplied (2 Pet. 1:10).
      It is thought that this judgment refers to the destruction of Jerusalem.
      Read Matthew 24:22, where Jesus spoke of this destruction and see
      what He had to say regarding being saved from such.

      a.   Are the righteous the same as the elect? _____

      b.   Regarding "judgment" in this verse: "Judgment (*krima*) as used
           here, denotes severe trial. The house of God is the family of
           God, the church (1 Tim. 3:15). The meaning is that the time when
           severe trial would fall upon the church was at hand" (W—119).
           Does this make the passage easier to understand? _____
           "The significance is, if the church, which is ever the object of
           God's care, is soon to fall into trial and sore persecution, how
           much greater must be the misery and wretchedness of those
           who do not rely on the Lord, and are thus without the comforting
           assurances of the gospel" (W—110)?

      c.   Thayer says the word for "scarcely" means "with difficulty." "It does
           not suggest doubt as to the outcome; only wonder that such a
           thing is possible! ... The 'judgment' (verse 17) which drew near
           would be so severe that even the pure and good would with great
           difficulty escape the destruction which it threatened ... We hence
           conclude that the salvation of the 'righteous' alluded to by Peter ...
           was deliverance from complete destruction in the persecution

which swept over the world in connection with the destruction of the temple and annihilation of the Jewish state in Jerusalem" (W—120-121).

d.   Since these verses are difficult to understand, I offer the comments of one other, James MacKnight, who gives the text along with his running commentary:

"17 Indeed the time is come, that the punishment to be inflicted on the Jews as a nation, for their crimes from first to last, must begin at you Jewish Christians, now become the house of God. And if it begins first at us, who are so dear to God on account of our faith in His Son, what will the end be of those Jews who obey not the gospel of God?

18 And when God thus punishes the nation, if the righteous Jews who believe in Christ with difficulty can be saved, where will the ungodly and the sinful part of the nation shew themselves saved from the divine vengeance?

19 In thus punishing the Jews God is just: Wherefore, let even the Gentile Christians who suffer with them in Judea by the will of God, use no unlawful means for preserving themselves, but commit their own lives to him in well-doing, as to a faithful Creator who can and will most certainly restore their lives to them at the resurrection" (M—624).

13.   If God's elect must so suffer in this world, how shall it be for "them that obey not the gospel", or the "ungodly" and the "sinner" at the final judgment" (2 Thess. 1:7-9) _____

_____

14.   What has one who is willing to suffer as a Christian committed unto God? _____

15.   What did Paul say about "suffer" and "committed" (2 Tim. 1:12)?

_____

The First Epistle of Peter: Chapter 5

RESPONSIBILITIES OF ELDERS (VS. 1-4)

1. What other words are used with reference to the office (work) of elders? (A total of four terms. Check the following references: Acts 20:28; Eph. 4:11; 1 Tim. 3:1; 1 Tim. 4:14).

    a. _____   b. _____

    c. _____   d. _____

2. What does "exhort" mean? _____

3. What three things did Peter say regarding himself? _____
    _____

4. In verse 2 what two things are the elders charged to do? _____
    _____

5. What phrase limits or restricts the feeding and overseeing done by the elders? _____

    a. Why did Paul leave Titus in Crete (Titus 1:5)? _____
        _____

    b. What does Acts 14:23 tell us about elders? _____
        _____
        Does this mean that when there are two or more churches in the same city, each church is to have elders? _____

    c. Is the instruction in 1 Peter 5 in harmony with Acts 14:23? _____

    d. Do elders have any authority to feed or oversee the flock of God in any other church than the church where they are elders? _____
        Suppose the church where they are elders is supporting a preacher in another place and the church there is new, can they

oversee that church until some men there are qualified to be elders? _____

e. Do elders have the authority to oversee the monies, or part of the monies, of any church other than the church where they are elders? _____ Are they to oversee any of the members of some other church? _____ Should members of another church be overtaken in error, can the elders teach them? THINK! _____

6. What three things are said regarding the oversight the elders are to take? There is a negative and a positive in each charge.

NOT	BUT
a. _____	_____
b. _____	_____
c. _____	_____

7. Elders are to serve willingly. Would it be right to coerce one who did not want to serve as an elder to accept the appointment? _____ "In the first age, when the profession of the gospel exposed men to persecution, and when the persecution fell more especially on the bishops, it may be easily imagined, that some who were appointed to that office, would undertake it unwillingly; perhaps, because they were to suffer. In such cases, the apostle very properly advised persons to decline the office" (M—625).

8. Not "for filthy lucre" (money) and not "as being lords" (power): Does this infer that some might want to be elders because of money and/or power? _____

9. In what way do you think an elder should be an example to the flock?
    _____

10. Who is the "chief Shepherd" (John 10:11)? _____

11. As shepherds, the elders are really "under shepherds." Read Hebrews 13:17 and tell what they must do. _____
    Unto whom must they give account? _____

12.   What shall the elders receive from the chief Shepherd? _____

13.   After studying all these passages regarding elders in the church, do
       you believe it is God's will that there be elders in every church? _____
       If the majority in a local church would rather have the "business
       meeting" type of rule, majority rule, than to have elders appointed, do
       you think that would be better? _____

REGARDING MAJORITY RULE

When Foy E. Wallace, Jr. was editor of the *Gospel Advocate* in the early '30s,
he had a very timely article on majority rule. He wrote,

"Considered from the scriptural viewpoint, majority rule violates many of
the principles of the apostolic teaching. In support of this statement, we
offer the following indictments against this deadly infection.

First: it is not discriminate between experience and inexperience, nor
regard knowledge as anything. It thus violates the New Testament principle
that some are more capable of discernment, possessing more knowledge
than others, and should teach while others of less experience and
knowledge should be taught (Hebrews 5:12-14).

Second: It makes the elders subject of the church instead of the church
subject to the elders, and reverses the New Testament principle: 'Obey
them that have the rule over you and submit yourselves ...' (Hebrews 13:17).

Third: It is the parent of the ballot, or vote, and becomes the occasion
of politics, electioneering, instructing children and young people how to
vote—all of which results in division (1 Cor. 1:10).

Fourth: It encourages preachers to disregard the elders and cater to the
wishes of the majority in the church. Thus, it has come to pass that any
preacher of average ability and personality can work up a sentiment against
the elders in almost any church and with the 'majority rule' doctrine divide
the church, in a flagrant violation of the New Testament command to 'know
(recognize) them which labor among you, and are over you in the Lord, and
admonish you; and to esteem them very highly in love for their works sake.
And be at peace among yourselves' (1 Thess. 5:12-13).

Fifth: It breeds anarchy in the church. Leaves the church in a state of
uncertainty without permanent leadership, and is against the New
Testament admonition to the elders to oversee the church (Acts20:28).

Sixth: The demand for majority rule always comes from the uninformed and unruly element in the church, not from the pious, consecrated people who are contented to worship God in spirit and in truth (1 Peter 5:5).

Seventh: Finally, and in short, the majority rule heresy is too political to be scriptural. Politics in government is bad, but in religion it's sad" (Via *Gospel News*, Vol. 26, No. 8, August, 1987).

RESPONSIBILITIES FOR ALL (VS. 5-11)

1.   Since the elders are to oversee, what are the younger to do? _____

_____

Compare Heb. 13:17 _____

_____

Note: The word "likewise" (5) means, "for the like reason," and since the elders had been exhorted to fulfill their responsibilities so that they might "receive a crown of glory that fadeth not away," for this like reason the younger are to fulfill their responsibilities that they might "receive a crown of glory."

2.   Does this mean submit to the elders regardless of what they demand?

_____

Does it mean to submit to them when they are serving in harmony with the word of the Lord? _____

3.   Subjecting or submitting one to another shows that brethren are clothed with what? _____

Note: "Clothed" is from a word which means "a white cloak used by slaves. Whitby says it was a frock put over the rest of the clothes; and that the apostles' meaning is, 'that humility should be visible over all other Christian virtues, in our whole behavior'" (M—625).

"Furthermore, used figuratively here, the meaning is, 'Tie on humility like a slave's apron.' The saints were thus to array themselves in humility; to tie it on securely like a garment so that it might never fall away. So arrayed, they were to regard no service as too menial or lowly, no task too small for them to perform. When Peter penned these words, he must have had a vivid mental picture of the Lord's action when he tied a towel about him and washed the disciples' feet, (John 13:10-17)" (W—128-129).

    a.   What are some works Christians may do that will show humility?

    _____

    _____

4.   How does God act toward the proud? _____
    What does He give to the humble? _____

5.   Christians must humble themselves under what? _____

6.   What is "the mighty hand of God"? _____

    _____

7.   How does one show that he had humbled himself under the mighty hand of God? By humble obedience to God's word? _____
    Or by refusing to do what God commands? _____

8.   What will God do for those who humble themselves under His hand?

    _____

    What did Jesus say about exalting self and being humble (Matt. 23:12)?

    _____

9.   Why should Christians cast their cares upon the Lord? _____
    How many cares should we cast upon Him? _____

    a.   How did Jesus illustrate God's care for His children? (Matt. 7:9-11)

       _____

    b.   Does God know that we have need of many things in this life? (See Matt. 6:32) _____ Is it right to ask God for things that we need? (Cf. Matt. 6:11)_____

10.   Who is the adversary of God's people? _____

    a.   How is he described in this verse? _____

    b.   What is he seeking? _____

    c.   In view of this, what two things did Peter charge the disciples to be? _____

11. How must Christians treat the devil? _____
     See James 4:7. Is this instruction the same? _____

12. How are Christians to resist the devil? By compromising the faith, or
     by being steadfast in the faith? _____

13. What did Peter say about the brethren? _____

14. What four things did Peter say God would do for the saints after they
     had suffered a while? _____
     _____

15. How did Peter refer to God? _____
     When we are saved will it be by our suffering or by His grace (See Eph.
     2:8)? _____

16. What should be given unto God "for ever and ever"? _____
     Read Ephesians 3:21 and Matthew 5:16 and tell how we give glory unto
     God. _____

THE FAREWELL (VS. 12-14)

1. What did Peter say he had done through Silvanus? _____

2. Why had Peter written this letter? _____

3. In the King James Version the words "church that" (13) are in italics,
    indicating that they were not in the original, but were added by the
    translators. The NASB and the NKJV read "She who is in Babylon."
    "She" probably refers to a sister who is not named. What is said of
    her? _____

4. In what sense was Marcus a son of Peter? _____

5. How were brethren to greet one another? (Cf. Rom. 16:16) _____
    _____

6. Peter bids peace to who? _____

7. How many are in Christ (Gal. 3:27)? _____

The Second Epistle of Peter: Chapter 1

There is a different tone in this letter than in the first letter by Peter, which had much to say about the hope of God's people. This one assures the faithful of an entrance into the heavenly kingdom (1:11), but warns again and again of false teachers and false doctrine, which, if believed and followed, would cause God's people to lose their inheritance. Peter writes to stir up the minds of brethren and make them remember the words of the holy prophets, apostles and the Lord (3:1-2).

THE GREETING (VS. 1-4)

1. How does Peter speak of himself? _____

    a. What determines whether one is a servant of Christ (Rom. 6:16)?

    _____

    b. What did Jesus say about those who will be great in His kingdom (Matt. 20:26-27)? _____

    c. In your judgment was Peter great in the kingdom? _____ Was he a faithful servant of Christ? _____

    d. What is required for one to be an apostle of Christ (Acts 1:21-22)?

    _____

2. To whom is this letter addressed? _____

    a. How had they obtained that faith? _____

3. To whom had Peter addressed the first letter (1 Peter 1:2)? _____

    _____

    a. What is the difference between the elect and them of "like precious faith?" _____

    b. Think about the word "precious." How would you define it? _____

    _____

"Faith is called precious, because it is more essential to men's happiness than all the things they esteem most precious." (M—630)

What are some things men hold as precious? _____

_____

c.   What makes faith a precious thing? _____

4.   How are grace and peace multiplied? _____

5.   Peter said, "His divine power has given unto us" what? _____

_____

a.   Life and godliness means godly living. Do you believe God has given unto men all things necessary for godly living? _____

b.   Peter said, His divine power has given unto "us" all things. Who are the "us" in this passage? And who are the "ye" or "you"? The apostle says, God has "given unto us" these things, "that by these ye might be…" etc. The "us" refers to Peter and the other apostles unto whom God had given "all things," and the "you" to those unto whom Peter addresses the letter. Consider the following:

False teachers were coming among brethren, Peter assures them "that Christ had given to His apostles everything necessary to qualify them for leading mankind to a godly life, and for making them partakers of the divine nature. He had bestowed on them inspiration to know the true doctrines of the gospel, and authority to declare them to the world" (M—630).

Who had received the promise from the Lord, "He will guide you into all truth" (John 16:13)? _____

Did all of those included in "you" (4) receive this promise from the Lord? _____

The gospel, the great salvation, was first spoken by whom (See Heb. 2:3)? _____

Then it "was confirmed unto us by them that heard him," the apostles. Do you agree? _____

    c.   Is it safe to conclude that the apostles were "guided into all truth"? _____

    d.   Does this necessarily infer that the so-called latter day revelations of the nineteenth and twentieth centuries do not pertain to life and godliness? _____

    e.   Read 2 Timothy 3:16-17. Into what will the scripture, given by inspiration of God, furnish "the man of God"? _____

    f.   Do these verses teach the sufficiency of God's word as revealed in apostolic days? _____

6.   All things that pertain to life and godliness are given "through the _____ of him that hath called us."

    a.   How is this knowledge obtained? _____

7.   How did Peter describe the promises that are given (NKJV reads "have been given") to us? _____

    a.   What are these promises? _____

    b.   What makes these promises great? _____

    c.   Why are these promises precious? _____

8.   By these (things God has given) we become partakers of what? _____
_____

The word translated "nature" "signifies the nature (i.e. the natural powers or constitution) of a person or thing" (Vine). Human nature is the natural power or constitution of being a part of human-kind (Cf. Eph. 2:3). Divine nature would be the natural power of constitution of divine beings. Christians partake of the divine nature, not by miraculous outpouring, but by the knowledge of His word.

9.   We know the nature of a human because we are human and we observe other humans. But how can we know the nature of a divine being? _____
_____

a.   How was God (divine being) "manifest in the flesh" (1 Tim. 3:16)?

_____

b.   When we study the life of Jesus, what He did, how He reacted in the various situations, does this show us the divine nature?_____

c.   Did Jesus always do and say what the Father would have done and said had He been in the flesh (John 14:7-11)? _____
Jesus said, "He that hath seen me hath seen _____."

d.   What does Hebrews 1:3 tell us about the image of Christ and God the Father? _____

e.   Peter told Christians that Jesus left us an example and we should follow His steps (1 Pet. 2:21). When we follow His steps are we partaking of His divine nature? _____

10.   Contrasting human and divine nature, listed below are several incidents that may occur in one's life. Following each of these, tell what is the natural human nature toward the incident and the divine nature toward the incident.

Incident (Matt. 5:38-45)	Human Nature	Divine Nature
Smite thee	_____	_____
Take coat	_____	_____
Compel to go a mile	_____	_____
Asks of thee	_____	_____
Enemy	_____	_____
Them that curse you	_____	_____
Them that hate you	_____	_____
Them that despitefully use you	_____	_____
Them that persecute you	_____	_____

Now complete this quotation of verse 45: "That ye may be the _____ of your _____ which is in heaven." Do children partake of the nature of their parents? THINK! _____

11. Christ exemplified the divine nature. Read 1 Peter 2:23 and tell how He was treated and how He reacted.

    a. When He was _____, He _____

    b. When He _____, He _____

12. Tell how Christ acted under these circumstances:

    a. When His enemies hated Him? _____

    b. When His enemies cursed Him? _____

    c. When He was persecuted? _____

    d. Did He hold a grudge? _____ Did He try to get even? _____

13. Now, go back to the text in 2 Peter 1:4, that "ye might be partakers of the divine nature, having escaped the _____ that is in the world through _____." Were these "the elect?"_____

14. Read Colossians 3:9-10, where Paul speaks to those who are "risen with Christ" (Col. 3:1).

    a. Do those things that are "put off" pertain to human nature or to divine nature? _____

    b. What were they to put on? _____

    c. How is this new man renewed after the image of Him that created him? _____

    d. After being renewed in knowledge, what were they to put on?

       _____

       Do these things pertain to human or divine nature? _____

    e. How did Paul refer to those who were to "put on" the new man (12)? _____

GROWING IN GRACE – THE CHRISTIAN GRACES (VS. 5-11)

1. "And beside this," or "for this very reason" (NKJV), referring to those things mentioned in verses 1-4, they were charged to add to what?

   _____

    a.   Do all Christians have faith? _____

    b.   Additions to faith must be made with all _____

2.   There are seven things to be added to faith. These are often called "Christian graces." List and define these seven things. (Compare with NKJV and NASB.)

    a.   _____

    b.   _____

    c.   _____

    d.   _____

    e.   _____

    f.   _____

    g.   _____

3.   "If these things be in you and abound" what is the result? _____
_____

4.   How is "he that lacketh these things" described?_____
_____

    a.   What is it that he cannot see? _____

    b.   Read 2 Corinthians 4:16-18. Paul speaks of two men. Who are they?
_____

       What did he call the "things which are seen"? _____
       and the "things which are not seen"? _____

5.   The one who is "blind and cannot see afar off: has forgotten" what?
_____

    a.   What is the meaning of "purged"? _____

    b.   Is this one concerned with things temporal or eternal? _____

6.   Unto what should Christians "give diligence"? _____
_____

How can this calling and election be made sure? _____

_____

7.   If you add these things to your faith, and abound ("and are increasing" NASB), what is the result? _____

8.   For those of you who do not stumble or fall, "an entrance shall be ministered unto you abundantly" into what? _____

    a.   Is this the same as "Receiving the end of your faith, even the salvation of your souls" (1 Pet. 1:9)? _____

REMEMBER THESE THINGS – SOURCE OF OUR KNOWLEDGE (VS. 12-21)

1.   Of what would Peter not "be negligent?"_____

    a.   Had they heard these things before? _____

    b.   In what were they to be established?_____

2.   What is "this tabernacle" of verses 13-14? _____
    Compare with NASB _____ and the NKJV _____

3.   What did Peter think it was right for him to do as long as he lived?

_____

4.   What did Peter say must shortly come to pass? _____
    What does this mean? _____

    a.   Whom did he say had showed him this? _____

    b.   Read John 21:18-19. What was Jesus telling Peter?_____

_____

5.   How could those of "like precious faith" have these things in remembrance after Peter's decease? _____

    a.   From whom did Peter receive the words he preached and wrote (See John 16:13)? _____

6.   What did Peter say "we have made known unto you"? _____

_____

7.   In making this known what had they "not followed"? _____
     Check the following references and tell what is said about fables.

     a.   1 Timothy 1:4 _____

     b.   1 Timothy 4:7 _____

     c.   2 Timothy 4:4 _____

     d.   Titus 1:13-14 _____

     e.   How should Christians feel about any of the commandments of
          men (Col. 2:21-22)? _____

8.   Who is the "we" of verse 16? _____
     Of what were they "eye witnesses"? _____

9.   Notice that in verses 12-15 Peter is saying "I" will or will not, but in
     verses 16-19 he changes to "we." Who was with Peter when they heard
     a voice from heaven (See Matt. 17:1-5)? _____
     _____

10. What did the voice they heard say? _____

11. Who received "honor and glory" from God the Father on that day?
     _____ How did He receive this? _____
     Would it be "honor and glory" unto you should God recognize you
     as one of His children? _____ How did John speak of men being
     called sons of God (1 John 3:1)? _____

12. What did Peter say we have? _____
     Compare with NKJV and NASB. How do they read? _____
     _____
     This seems to be a better rendering of it, for the Mount of
     Transfiguration scene, which they witnessed, confirmed what the
     prophets of old had prophesied, i.e., a Savior is coming, a new
     covenant will be given, and many other prophecies too numerous to
     mention here. Do you agree? _____

13. Unto what were they to take heed? _____
     _____

14. In a figure of speech the prophetic word is compared to what?

    _____

    a. Read Psalm 119:105. What is the word of God called? _____

    b. Peter said this light is to shine until when (19)? _____

    _____

    c. Who is "the bright and morning star" (Rev. 22:16)? _____
    The days of the prophetic word were as a dark place, the word
    of the prophets as a light ("lamp" NASB) shining in that dark
    place, until the day dawns (a time of more light) and the day-star
    ("morning star" NASB) rises. The coming of Christ and His word
    would bring light to a world of darkness. Do you agree? _____

15. What did Peter want them to know? _____

    _____

    a. Does this mean it is impossible for one to privately interpret or
    understand the word of God? _____

    b. Is this speaking of the word that was given? Or of how the
    prophecy came?_____

16. About the prophecy: How did it not come? _____
    How did it come? _____
    Note: The apostle has emphasized three things: "That the prophetic
    word is a product of inspiration; that it was delivered by men who
    spake from God; and that those who thus spoke were moved to do so
    by the Holy Spirit" (W—163).

17. Can these same things be said of the words of the apostles and other
    writers of the books of the New Testament? _____
    Can they be said of the writings of Joseph Smith _____ Ellen G.
    White? _____ The twentieth century "apostles" of the Mormon
    Church? _____ the Pope of the Catholic Church? _____ Any of the
    present-day preachers or writers? _____

    a. Paul said, "the gospel which was preached of me is not after"
    whom? (Gal. 1:11) _____

He also said, "My preaching was not with enticing words of
_____ _____" (1 Cor. 2:4), "that your faith should
not stand in the _____ of _____ but in the power of
_____" (1 Cor. 2:5).

b.   How did Paul and other apostles receive that which they
preached (Gal. 1:12)? _____

c.   When Jesus promised the apostles that the Spirit would come unto
them, into what was He to guide them (John 16:13)? _____

d.   Read 1 Corinthians 2:12-13 and tell what Paul and other apostles
received? _____
Why did they receive the Spirit? _____
What did they speak? _____

e.   Read Ephesians 3:3-4. How did God make known His will unto the
apostles and prophets? _____
What did they speak? _____
Can we read their words and understand? _____
Conclusion: Were the apostles of Christ "holy men of God"?_____
Did they speak as they were moved by the Holy Spirit?_____
Is their message given by the inspiration of God?_____
Are those things taught by the apostles of Christ just as
authoritative and as binding as those things taught by Jesus
Himself? _____

The Second Epistle of Peter: Chapter 2

WARNING AGAINST FALSE TEACHERS (VS. 1-3)

1. Were there false prophets among the people of God in Old Testament days? _____ Were these "holy men of God"? _____ Did they speak by inspiration? _____

    a. Read Isaiah 9:13-16. What did he say some prophets would teach?

        _____

        What did the leaders cause the people to do? _____

        _____

    b. What did the Lord say about such false prophets (Jer. 14:14)?

        _____

2. Peter declared that there were false prophets, "even as there shall be" what? _____

3. What would these false teachers do? _____

    _____

    a. What are heresies? _____

    b. What word describes these "heresies?" _____

4. How would these false teachers "bring in" their heresies? _____

    _____

    a. Would these teachers be teaching some truth? _____

    b. The world translated "privily" or "secretly" literally means, "to slip by the side of, and indicates that these teachers had artfully and slyly introduced their false doctrines by the side of the truth in such fashion as to deceive those who had accepted them" (W—163).

5.   What particular false doctrine would some teach? _____

_____

    a.   Unto whom do all Christians belong (1 Cor. 6:19-20)? _____

    b.   What price was paid for our redemption (1 Pet. 1:18)? _____

6.   The deity of Christ has been denied since the First Century A.D., but men who spoke by the Spirit of God declared Him to be the Son of God.

    a.   What did John say about Christ in 1 John 4:2, 15? _____

    _____

    b.   Are there false teachers of our day who deny the deity of Jesus? _____
    Who are some of them?_____

7.   What do such false teachers bring upon themselves?_____

    a.   How does John describe the place where the false prophets shall be (Rev. 20:10)? _____

8.   How does Peter describe the ways of these false prophets (2)?

_____

    a.   What does "pernicious" mean? _____
    The NASB reads "sensuality." What does this mean? _____

    _____

    The NKJV says, "destructive ways"; is this in harmony with the preceding statement, verse 1? _____
    "These teachers ... made religion of lusts, and ... preached the gospel of libertinism" (W—163). Such leads to eternal destruction.

    b.   What did the wise man say about the "way that seemeth right unto a man" (Prov. 16:25)? _____

9.   Because of these false teachers, and their followers, what will some say about "the way of truth"?_____

    a.   Do some still speak evil of the way of truth because of the ungodly and immoral lives of many who claim to be Christians?_____

10.   What did Peter say these false teachers will make of you? _____

    a.   They will do this by covetousness. What is covetousness? _____

       _____

    b.   What kind of words will they speak? _____

    c.   Compare the NASB _____
       and the NKJV _____

11.   God has declared the destruction that shall come to false teachers.

    a.   What did Paul say of them in Philippians 3:18-19? _____

       _____

    b.   What two figures are used by Peter to show that their destruction
       is certain? _____

       _____

       Be prepared to discuss the meaning.

DESTRUCTION OF FALSE TEACHERS AND DELIVERANCE OF THE RIGHTEOUS (VS. 4-11)

Verses 4-10a are one very long sentence, assuring us that the Lord knows how to deliver the godly and to reserve the unjust unto the day of judgment.

1.   There are three examples of God not sparing the unjust. List them.

    a.   Verse 4_____

    b.   Verse 5 _____

    c.   Verse 6 _____

2.   List two examples of God's ability to deliver the godly.

    a.   Verse 5_____

    b.   Verse 7 _____

3.   What do you think those who received this letter from Peter would learn from these examples? _____

    _____

"The angels that sinned" (4) have been the center of much discussion. Peter does not tell us what their sin was, or when they sinned or how many of them sinned. Thus, any thing relating to their sin would be assumption and worth nothing. An interesting comment,

"Angels are created beings, 'sent forth to do service for the sake of them that shall inherit salvation' (Heb. 1:14). They are moral creatures and answerable to God for their conduct, though apparently outside the redemptive provisions of grace (Heb. 2:16). Thus, when they sin, they are beyond the possibility of salvation. These, despite their rank, the honorable position they occupied, and the holiness they possessed when created, sinned, and were not spared ... Inasmuch as it is inconceivable that God created them wicked, the following conclusions seem certain: (a) they were originally holy; (b) they sinned; (c) The occasion of their sin was abandoning their 'proper habitation'; (d) as a result they were thrust down to a place of bondage" (W—165-166).

a.   If "God spared not" such angels when they sinned, will He spare false teachers? _____

b.   Where were these angels cast? _____
Note: The word hell in this verse is from "tartarus" and is not found elsewhere in the Greek New Testament. It is evidently the compartment of hades where the wicked are kept until the day of judgment (See Luke 16:23-26).

c.   Peter says these angels are reserved unto what? _____

4.   Unto what does the term "old world" refer? _____

5.   What did God bring upon "the world of the ungodly"? _____

6.   Whom did God deliver or save from that world? _____

a.   How is Noah described in verse five? _____

b.   What is righteousness (Psa. 119:172)? _____

c.   Was Noah preaching righteousness to an ungodly world? _____
Do you suppose the world loved Noah? _____

Was he successful as a preacher of righteousness? THINK! _____
Does being faithful as a preacher depend upon the number of
those converted? _____ Does it depend upon preaching God's
word and pleasing God (See Gal. 1:10)? _____

d.   "Noah was a just man and perfect in his generations" (Gen. 6:9),
"a righteous man, blameless in his time; Noah walked with God"
(NASB). He was righteous and he preached righteousness, so he
must have practiced what he preached. Do you agree? _____

(1) Shouldn't every preacher practice righteousness? _____

(2) If he practices what he preaches will everybody love him and
follow his teaching? _____

(3) Are there any preachers who do not practice what they
preach? _____

e.   Remember the point: "The Lord knoweth how to deliver the
godly." Can you see how Peter is emphasizing that point? _____

7.   If God spared not the ungodly world then, will He spare the ungodly
world of today? _____

8.   What kind of people lived in Sodom and Gomorrah (Gen. 18:20)?
_____
How does Jude describe them (Jude 7)? _____
_____

9.   How did Abraham try to get God to spare these cities (Gen. 18:23-33)?
_____

10. How did God destroy the cities?_____

a.   What did Peter say God turned the cities into? _____

b.   Unto whom has God made them an example? _____
_____

c.   Remember the point: "The Lord knoweth how ... to reserve the
unjust unto the day of judgment." When you read of Sodom and

Gomorrah can you see that point? _____

11.   Who was delivered from Sodom? _____

    a.   What word describes the Lord (Cf. NKJV)? _____

    b.   How did living in such a wicked city make Lot feel? _____
       The word in the NKJV is "tormented." Should our souls be
       tormented by the unlawful deeds of those of the world? _____
       Regarding righteous Lot, "Though in the midst of extreme
       wickedness, (a) Lot was not corrupted by it; (b) he did not become
       indifferent to it; (c) He was daily concerned about it" (W—169).
       Can we learn something from this man? _____
       What? _____

12.   Having studied these examples do you really believe that "the Lord
    knows how to deliver the godly out of temptation"? _____

    a.   Does the promise say God will keep trials from coming to the
       godly? ____ Does it promise a miracle to deliver them from
       temptation? _____ Read 1 Corinthians 10:12-13. When temptation
       comes, what does God always make? _____

13.   Do the three examples cited by Peter prove that God is able to
    "reserve the unjust unto the day of judgment to be punished?"_____
    An interesting comment, "This spoils a wishful-thinking notion that 'a
    man will get all of his "hell" in this life.' Wicked men as well as wicked
    angels will not be given their final sentence until the judgment at the
    last day" (Z—274).

14.   God will reserve the punishment of all wicked men unto judgment,
    but "chiefly" or "especially" (NKJV) whom?_____
    _____

    a.   The reference is to the false teachers (11). How does Peter say
       they are walking? _____

    b.   What three expressions describe these false teachers?
       _____
       _____

DEPRAVITY OF FALSE TEACHERS (VS. 12-17)

These verses describe the vile, corrupt condition of the false teachers. Read these verses a couple times (at least), then read them in the NKJV, and complete the following exercise, which will give emphasis to the condition of such false teachers.

1. "But these...

    a. "Speak evil of _____ "

        (1) Should one speak evil of things he does not know? _____

    b. "Will utterly _____ "

        (1) Shall each of us reap as he has sowed (Gal. 6:7)? _____

    c. "Shall receive the reward of _____ "

        (1) What are the wages of sin (Rom. 6:23)? _____
             Compare Revelation 20:14 _____

2. "They are...

    a. "Spots and _____ "

        (1) "Sporting themselves with _____ "
             ("Carousing in their own deceptions" NKJV)

        (2) "Having eyes full of _____
             and that cannot cease from _____ "

        (3) "Beguiling unstable _____ "
             What does this mean? _____

        (4) Cursed_____

    b. How is Christ described in 1 Peter 1:19? _____
        What kind of church will Christ present unto himself (Eph. 5:27)?

        _____

    c. What did Jesus say about the man who looks upon a woman and
        lusts after her (Matt. 5:28)? _____

        _____

3.   They have …

  a.   "An heart … exercised (or "trained" NKJV) in _____ "

    (1) Each of us is what he puts into his heart. These had their hearts trained in covetous practices. How did they train their hearts? _____

  b.   "Forsaken the_____ "

    (1) What had Peter called the right way back in verse 2?

        _____

        Does this imply that these false teachers were once in the right way?_____

  c.   "Gone … the way of _____ "

    (1) The student should be familiar with that incident. Read Num. 22:1-41. What was the sin of Balaam? _____

    (2) How were these false teachers like Balaam? _____

    (3) Is it possible that we have such false teachers today?_____

4.   "These are …

  a.   "Wells _____ "

    (1) What are wells or "springs" (NKJV) without water? _____

  b.   "Clouds _____ "

    (1) What does this mean? _____

5.   Conclusion: Unto what are these persons reserved? _____

  a.   Is the Lord able to reserve the ungodly unto the day of judgment to punish them? _____

HOW FALSE TEACHERS DECEIVE (VS. 18-22)

1.   What kind of words do false teachers use? _____

2.   Through what do they allure people? _____

3.   Who do they allure? _____
     Those "who live in error" refers to the heathen who knew not the
     Lord.

4.   What did the false teachers promise? _____
     "These evil workers held out the prospect of a life free from the
     restraints of law. Yet while emphasizing the good fortune of being
     'free men' they were themselves a group of slaves. Not to temporal or
     literal masters it is true, but to the harsh master of sin" (Z—275).

5.   How did Peter prove that the false teachers were really in bondage?

     _____

6.   From what had the false teachers escaped? _____
     How had they escaped such? _____

7.   If, after escaping the corruption of the world, "they are again
     entangled therein, and overcome," what is their condition? _____

     a.   Does this mean that a "back-slider" cannot repent? THINK! _____

     b.   What makes their condition worse? _____

          _____

          "The reason the backslider is in a worse state than the alien
          sinner is that his heart has been hardened by the experiences
          and will be less favorable to the truth." (Z—276).

8.   What did Peter say would be "better for them"? _____

     _____

     "It would have been better for them never to have known the right
     way in view of their subsequent apostasy, for (a) in this event they
     would not have brought reproach upon the cause of Christ; (b) they
     would not have fallen to such a level of depravity as that which now
     characterized them; and (c) they would not suffer as great punishment
     in the last day, since with increased knowledge comes an increase of
     responsibility and consequently greater condemnation for those who
     do not avail themselves of the advantage afforded them. (Luke 12:47,
     48)" (W—177-178).

9.   What two animals are used to illustrate the condition of such false
     teachers? _____

     a.   What does Proverbs 26:11 say? _____

          _____

     b.   The proverb of the sow was one known to those of Peter's time,
          learned by observation. Does this proverb help you see the point
          being made? _____

     c.   What animal did Jesus associate with the use of that which is holy
          and valuable (Matt. 7:6)? _____
          "Cited in this proverb are two beasts held in greatest contempt
          in all Oriental lands. The dog is a scavenger, and the swine is
          regarded as an abomination ... The proverb was one of general
          currency when Peter wrote. It should be observed that in both
          instances the animal was changed. That each returned to its
          former offensive habits does not alter the fact that a change
          had occurred. Advocates of the doctrine of the impossibility of
          apostasy, in an effort to avoid the obvious force of the passage,
          insist that the dog remained a dog, the sow a sow. Such is not the
          point of the proverb. The dog had ejected that which was foul; the
          sow had been washed. That each returned to its former manner
          of life reveals that the old nature returned. Peter cites the proverb
          as an illustration of that which had occurred in the lives of these
          men who, though they had escaped the corruption of the world
          through the knowledge of Christ, had become entangled again
          therein, and overcome, and their last state was thus worse than
          the first" (W—178).

The Second Epistle of Peter: Chapter 3

THE WORD OF GOD IS SURE – CHRIST WILL COME AGAIN (VS. 1-13)

1. How does Peter address the brethren? _____

2. How do we know that those to whom this letter was written are the same as those to whom the first letter was addressed? _____
    _____

3. Make a comparison of how Peter addressed them in the first letter and in this one.

    a. In the first what are they called (1:2)? _____

    b. In the second how does he speak of them? _____

4. Why did Peter say he was writing this second epistle? _____
    _____

    a. Do Christians need to have their minds stirred up today? _____

    b. How did Peter speak of their minds? _____

    c. How are pure minds stirred up? _____

5. Of what did Peter want them to be mindful? _____
    _____

6. "Knowing this first" means, "this first understand" (See also 1:20), thus, before bringing up the subject of the coming of Christ, he reminds them that scoffers must come.

    a. What are scoffers?_____

7. When were these scoffers to come? _____

    a. What does the expression "the last days" mean? (See Acts 2:16-17; Joel 2:28). _____

8.   How does Peter describe these scoffers?_____

   a.   Does this mean they had more regard for themselves than for God? _____

   b.   What does John say about such men (1 John 2:19)? _____
   _____

9.   What were these scoffers saying? _____

10.   The second coming of Christ is a fundamental part of the doctrine of Christ and/or the apostles' doctrine.

   a.   Read John 14:1-3. What did Jesus promise? _____

   b.   Read Acts 1:10-11. Who declared that He shall come again? _____

   c.   What did Paul say about His coming (Phil. 3:20)? _____

   d.   Read 2 Peter 1:16. Did Peter teach the coming of the Lord?_____

11.   What reasoning did they use to prove that Christ is not coming again?
   _____

   a.   Did their argument prove that Christ is not coming again? _____

   b.   Had all things remained the same since the creation? NO! God had sent the flood to destroy sinful men, but they had forgotten that. Are false teachers often inconsistent? _____

12.   What did Peter say those scoffers were ignorant of or "willfully forget" (NKJV)?_____

   a.   By what did Peter say the heavens were of old? _____

   b.   The Genesis account of creation says over and over "and God said" (Gen. 1). Does Peter's statement agree with this? _____

   c.   How does Peter describe the earth (5)? _____

13.   "Whereby" or "by which" (NKJV) in verse 6 refers to "the water." What happened to that world that then was?_____

   a.   God said, "I, even I, do bring a flood of waters upon the earth"

(Gen. 6:17). Did He keep His word? _____

b. The word "perished" (from *apollumi*) means "to destroy" (Vine). "It was not annihilated, for such the word does not mean. The existing order was changed; the evils of the age were removed, and there emerged a new world cleansed from its former impurities" (W—183).

14.   By what power are the heavens and the earth which are now "kept in store"?_____

a. Does that mean God's word? _____

b. Unto what are the present heavens and earth being kept in store, or reserved? _____

c. Reserved "against" or "until" (NKJV) what? _____
Note: The NASB says "destruction of ungodly men." It is the same word as "perished" in verse six, and "signifies to destroy utterly; the idea is not extinction but ruin, loss, not of being, but of well-being ... of the loss of well-being in the case of the unsaved hereafter" (Vine). Mr. Vine lists twelve passages where the word is used, one of which is 2 Peter 3:9.

"The word 'destruction' is identical in meaning with the verb 'perish' in the preceding verse. By this it is not meant that the ungodly will cease to exist, any more than the earth following the flood, existed no more. What is meant is that there will be a change in their condition attended by penal consequences as great as that which characterized the earth in the flood" (W—184).

These observations are pointed out because some teach that the destruction of the ungodly means complete annihilation of the wicked. Read 2 Thessalonians 1:7-9. What is the punishment of those who know not God and obey not the gospel? _____
_____

Not everlasting destruction, period! But everlasting destruction FROM what? _____

15.   Peter said, "beloved, be not ignorant of this one thing." What one thing? _____

   a.   Does this mean that with God it takes a thousand years to make a day? _____ Does it mean that time does not affect God as it does man? _____ Does it mean that the passing of time does not affect the promises and the threats of God? _____

   b.   With man, the longer the time that passes from the making of a promise to the keeping of it, the less likely he is to fulfill it. With man several things may occur with the passing of time. How would these affect his promise?

      (1) He may die. _____

      (2) He may forget his promise. _____

      (3) He might refuse to keep his promise. _____

      (4) Conditions may arise that make it impossible for him to keep it, such as_____

   c.   Can any of these things happen to God?_____

16.   What is the inevitable conclusion with reference to the promise of the Lord? _____

   a.   How is God toward us? _____

   b.   Does this account for His delay in fulfilling the promise? _____

   c.   What does God desire for all men? _____

   d.   What does He NOT desire for any man? _____

   e.   Is the longsuffering of God endless?_____

      (1) He was longsuffering in the days of Noah "while the _____ was a _____" (1 Pet. 3:20).

      (2) When God decided that He would destroy sinful man, how long was it before the flood came (Gen. 6:3)? _____

f. Since the delay in the coming of the Lord is because God is longsuffering, not wanting any to perish, does this necessarily imply that there will be no chance of salvation given after His return and the earth is destroyed? _____

g. Are there some who teach that there will be another opportunity given after death? _____ What does this make of their doctrine? _____

THE DAY OF THE LORD (VS. 10-13)

1. What is "the day of the Lord"? _____

    a. How did angels say He would come (Acts 1:9-11)? _____
    _____

    b. What did Jesus say would occur at His coming (John 5:28-29)?
    _____

    c. "The coming of our Lord Jesus Christ" and "the day of Christ" are the same, see how Paul refers to it:

    (1) 1 Corinthians 1:8 _____

    (2) Philippians 1:6 _____

    (3) 1 Thessalonians 5:2 _____

2. How shall He come? _____

    a. What does this mean? _____

    b. What did Jesus teach about His coming (Matt. 24:42-44)? _____
    _____

3. When Jesus comes what shall happen to ...

    a. The heavens? _____

    (1) What did Paul say about heaven (2 Cor. 12:2)? _____
    What is the third heaven? _____

(2) This "great noise" is an interesting expression. "The word thus translated is *rhoizedon*, an onomatopoeic term, in which the sound denotes the meaning. Its kindred noun, *rhodsos*, was used in classical Greek of the whizzing of an arrow, the whirring rush of wings, the sound of the wind, and the murmur of waters. Here it describes the crash of dissolving worlds and the tremendous roar of flames as they consume the earth" (W—186).

"The whistling of an arrow, signifies 'with rushing sound' as of roaring flames, and is used in 2 Peter 3:10, of the future passing away of the heavens" (Vine).

b.   The elements? _____

(1) What are the elements? "The elements from which all things have come, the material causes of the universe" (Thayer). Do you agree?_____

c.   The earth and the works that are in it?_____

(1) What are these works? _____

(2) "The earth is part of the same material universe ... but it is given special mention because it is where man lives at present, thus giving him serious warning of the fatal event" (Z—277).

d.   Read Matthew 24:35. What did Jesus say would come to pass?

_____

(1) Who knows and who does not know when this shall come to pass? _____

(2) How do we know these things shall come to pass?_____

_____

4.   Seeing then that all these things shall be dissolved, what kind of persons ought Christians be? _____

a.   What is another word for conversation?_____

b.   "What manner of persons" is literally, "of what country" (W—187). What did Paul say about our citizenship (Phil. 3:20)? _____

c.   In view of these things, upon what should we fix our attention (2 Cor. 4:18)? _____

5.   Christians should be "looking for and hasting" unto what? _____

_____

a.   The English word "hasting" means "to cause to hurry" and the word in this text means "to desire earnestly" (Vine). Do you think we should desire the Lord's coming? _____

b.   Is "the day of God" the same as "the day of the Lord" (10)? _____

6.   What does Peter reaffirm shall occur at "the coming of the day of God" (12)? _____

7.   For what do Christians look (13)? _____

a.   Why do we look for new heavens and a new earth? _____

_____

b.   Read Isaiah 65:17. What did God promise? _____

c.   What did John see (Rev. 21:1)? _____

8.   What kind of heavens and earth does Peter refer to (13)? _____

a.   According to Vine and other recognized authorities on N.T. words, there are different Greek words translated "new" in our English language. A study of these may help us on this point.

(1)   *Kainos*—"denotes new, of that which is unaccustomed or unused not new in time, but new as to form or quality, of different nature from what is contrasted as old."

(2)   *Neos*—"signifies new in respect of time."

(3)   *Prosphatos*—"originally signifying freshly slain, acquired the general sense of new, as applied to flowers, oil, misfortune, etc."

Note: *Kainos* is the word used of "the new" heavens and earth. If God had wanted to tell man that the new heavens and new earth were in respect of time, he would have used a different word. Does this help you have a better understanding of the new heavens and new earth?_____

b. "There are two words translated 'new' in the New Testament; one is prospective and indicates that which is young as opposed to old; the other is retrospective and points to that which is fresh in contrast to that which is worn out. It is the second of these (*kainos*) which is used here. The heavens and the earth which the apostle describes in this passage will be fresh and new and not worn and old, as are the heavens and the earth which now exist. In this new heaven and earth righteousness will dwell. Righteousness here contemplated will, therefore, be the abode of righteous and obedient people" (W—188).

9. Who and what shall dwell in the new heavens and new earth? _____
    True or False:
    _____ Righteousness dwells where righteous people live.
    _____ Righteousness will dwell in the new heavens and earth.
    _____ The new heavens and new earth will be the abode of the
            righteous, the people of God.

10. Woods says the new heavens and new earth is the same as heaven. The following is his reasoning:

    a. The present heavens and earth serve as a figure of the heavens and earth to follow.

    b. The words "heavens and earth" are not intended to embrace all of God's material universe, but only that portion where his people dwell.

    c. In the antitype, this limitation must be understood, and the words "new heaven and earth" must then be regarded as a designation of where his people dwell, and not a detailed description of the future abode.

d.   Heaven is the final abode of the people of God.

e.   Therefore, the phrase "new heavens and earth" must be understood as a designation of heaven! (W—189)

Note: References to Woods, Zerr, Vine and Thayer are made for your consideration and study, with no intention of making their words parallel to the words of the apostles and other inspired men.

BE STEADFAST (VS. 14-18)

1.   What are the things Christians look for? _____

2.   How should God's people be as they await the coming of these things? _____

a.   How did Peter express it in 2 Peter 1:10? _____
     _____

3.   Name three things that tell how we should be found of Him (14)?
     _____

a.   In peace with whom? _____

b.   What does it mean to be without spot? _____
     How is this possible (1 Jn. 1:7-9)? _____

c.   Define blameless. _____

4.   What is "the longsuffering of our Lord" (15)? _____
     How is it salvation? _____

5.   Unto whose writings did Peter refer? _____
     Does this reference show ...

a.   That Peter was acquainted with the writings of Paul? _____

b.   That those to whom he wrote were acquainted with them? _____

c.   That Peter considered the writings of Paul as inspired? _____

Can you see that each of these points is sustained in the passage? _____

6.   Of what "things" did Paul speak in his epistles? (16) _____

_____

a.   What did Peter say about "some things" Paul had written? _____

_____

b.   Who were those who did "wrest" or "twist" (NKJV) some of the things Paul had written? _____

c.   What was the result of such twisting of the scripture?_____

_____

Do you agree or disagree?

_____ (1) The destruction which results is due, not to the scripture or its writers, but to improper handling by men.

_____ (2) The passage does not teach that all scripture is hard or difficult to understand.

_____ (3) It does not lend support to the view that man needs an infallible interpreter of the scripture.

_____ (4) Some scripture is taught to be difficult to understand and evil men twist these scriptures for ungodly purposes.

_____ (5) The lesson, by implication, is that we should be on guard against any interpretation contrary to the general teaching of the Bible (See W—192).

7.   Of what were brethren to beware? _____

_____

a.   What does "beware" mean? _____

b.   Does this sound like "once saved always saved"? _____

8.   There is an old saying, "to be forewarned is to be forearmed." Were those who read this epistle forewarned of the danger of being led away from the Lord? _____ Are you forewarned?_____

    a.   How may some be led away? _____

_____

9.   To help avoid the danger of falling or being led away, in what are God's people to grow? _____

    a.   How can one grow in grace and knowledge (1 Peter 2:2)? _____

_____

10.   Unto whom is glory to be given both now and forever? _____

WHERE WILL THE NEW EARTH BE LOCATED?

Some teach that the present earth will be cleansed of all sin and the saved ones will live here forever (Jehovah's Witnesses). This has a strong appeal to people who already have strong ties to the present world and would like to live here forever in peace, without sin, etc. Others teach that Christ is coming to set up His kingdom on earth and reign for a thousand years and the redeemed ones will live with him.

Some final comments on the new earth are worthy of sharing:

"More than this we cannot, with our present store of information, know. Numerous questions men are disposed to raise regarding the matter it was not Peter's intention (or, for that matter, any inspired man's) to answer. Where will the new heavens and new earth be located? What will be the nature and characteristics of it? Are questions beyond our ken. It is sufficient for us to note that

    a.   The new heavens and earth will follow the destruction of the present heavens and earth.

    b.   The earth that will then be is not this one.

    c.   It is this earth which embodies the hopes and expectations of future kingdom advocates.

    d.   There is no hint of a reign of Christ on the earth which Peter describes.

    e.   Christ will have terminated his reign and delivered the kingdom to the Father before the events are accomplished which the apostle here details (1 Cor. 15:23ff).

    f.   There is, therefore, no support whatsoever in this passage for the premillennial theory" (W—189).

www.ingramcontent.com/pod-product-compliance
Lightning Source LLC
Chambersburg PA
CBHW060028050426
42448CB00012B/2911